D0111626

AUTHENTICITY

THOMAS DUBAY, S.M.

AUTHENTICITY

A Biblical Theology of Discernment

UPDATED EDITION

IGNATIUS PRESS   SAN FRANCISCO

Original edition published in 1977 by Dimension Books

Published with ecclesiastical approval
Revised edition printed with permission of the author

Cover art: Samuel Palmer, *Pear Tree in a Walled Garden*
Watercolor and gouache, 8¾ x 11⅛"
(Gift of Mr. & Mrs. Eugene V. Thaw, 1980.37.)
The Pierpont Morgan Library/Art Resource
New York, New York

Cover design by Roxanne Mei Lum

Published by Ignatius Press, San Francisco, 1997
ISBN 0–89870–619–x
Library of Congress catalogue number 96–78009
Printed in the United States of America ⊗

CONTENTS

II
POSSIBILITY OF DISCERNMENT

III
SIGNS OF THE HOLY SPIRIT

IV
VERIFICATION AND IMPLICATIONS

ABBREVIATIONS

AG   *Ad gentes divinitus,* Vatican Council II, Decree on the Missionary Activity of the Church
CCC   *Catechism of the Catholic Church*
DBT   *Dictionary of Biblical Theology,* edited by Xavier Léon-Dufour
GS   *Gaudium et spes,* Vatican Council II, Pastoral Constitution on the Church in the Modern World
LG   *Lumen gentium,* Vatican Council II, Dogmatic Constitution on the Church
JB   *Jerusalem Bible*
JBC   *Jerome Biblical Commentary,* ed. Raymond E. Brown, Joseph A. Fitzmyer, Roland E. Murphy (Englewood Cliffs, N.J.: Prentice-Hall, 1968)
NAB   *New American Bible*
NCE   *New Catholic Encyclopedia*
PO   *Presbyterorum ordinis,* Vatican Council II, Decree on the Ministry and Life of Priests
RSV   *Revised Standard Version*
SC   *Sacrosanctum concilium,* Vatican Council II, Constitution on the Sacred Liturgy

9

PREFACE

When the chips are down in life and death situations, philosophical relativism evaporates into thin air. The academic idea that objective, absolute certitude does not matter much, that value judgments about reality are roughly equivalent in worth, that theological dissent is on a par with magisterial teaching (the now dated "parallel magisteria" idea), all these notions are quietly abandoned when their proponents face some issue they consider of crucial importance. Suddenly they demand absolute, objective truth.

Though relativism in matters ethical and religious is widespread both in academic circles and in public education, and is spreading in popular culture, it is nonexistent when there is question of facing what people consider of drastic importance. No one embarking on a transatlantic flight, no matter how dogmatically he is committed to materialism in his academic tower or in his lectures and writings, will rest content with the news that airport personnel have conflicting views as to how much fuel the plane's tanks do or do not hold. He insists on objective certitude.

This book, therefore, continues to be pressingly relevant. It deals with how we find truth and how we may be sure that we have found it—as the inspired word deals with the question. It is about that kind of truth beside which all other human concerns pale in comparison. I refer, of course, to God and our reaching him in the eternal ecstasy of the beatific vision in risen body. Everything else is for the passing moment and soon dissolves into ashes, unless it has contributed in some manner to our unspeakable destiny.

These pages offer a detailed look at the divine recipe for discovering what the Lord has in store for us, and where on this planet we can find his road map. How do we discover, in the increasing welter of conflicting claims, what is the meaning of life, and what are we to think about the varying denials that there is a meaning? In this information age, we are threatened with suffocation by the media's avalanche of papers and periodicals, radio, film and television, cyberspace and the Internet. Where do ordinary people find the fresh air of ultimate reality and know with certitude that they have found it? No other question approaches this one for crucial importance. Consistent theism demands a cogent answer. No theist with a sound, consistent and reflecting mind is going to be content with value clarification and mere pragmatism.

The increasing polarization in the Church, now often touched with acrimony, is a complex phenomenon with a number of diverse causes and a complex of symptoms. Efforts to find a common ground among the main factions in our midst are commendable as long as they are realistic. If history makes anything clear, it is that unity in matters ethical and religious is impossible if efforts are based merely on the work of committees and study groups, on the proposals of position papers and the scheduling of meetings. They may occasion more cordial relations and diminish caricature and bitterness, but experience, past and present, declares their inadequacy for achieving the New Testament demand that we be of one mind regarding divine revelation and how it is to be interpreted.

Pursuit of a common ground among Christians in general and Catholics in particular is unreal precisely to the extent that it avoids addressing the problems sketched in this volume. Sad to say, we do not find these problems on the proposed agendas. Could it be that the answers given in the New Testament embarrass those with private agendas?

The questions in this discernment area that the Scriptures answer continue to be those that have troubled us for three or four decades. When and how does God speak? What are the conditions that ready a person to recognize divine truth and enable him to embrace it? Does the Lord allow for philosophical and religious relativism? How do we deal with the welter of conflicting interpretations of divine revelation? What keeps the faithful from being led astray? How can we know a genuine experience of God as distinguished from the illusions of subjectivity? What are we to think of illuminism, the age-old but foundationless conviction of enthusiasts that they have a privileged access to the divine mind, people who are so convinced that they possess divine light that contrary evidence makes not the least dent in their self-assurance? What is intellectual conversion, and how does it come about? What are the signs pointing to those who understand revelation rightly—and those who do not?

The correct answers to these questions, and others related to them, can be summarized by the one word, authenticity. Unless the two poles, of left and right, face and come to terms with these questions and the divine answers, there will be no common ground, no achieved oneness of mind, a oneness so insisted upon in the New

Testament. We hardly need to add that there will be little or no ecumenical progress.

As Hans Urs von Balthasar has happily noted, truth is symphonic. Musicians who, preferring their own personal interpretations of a master, tinker with the score or disregard the maestro ruin the melodic splendor of a Mozart concerto or a Beethoven symphony. What could be more obvious? Yet few seem to realize that those who bypass the divine score explored in this volume—or who reject the divinely appointed conductor—bring about the religious chaos we see all about us. Yes, indeed, truth is symphonic.

PREFACE TO THE FIRST EDITION

It is intriguing how most of us see what we want to see, hear what we want to hear, speak of what we love to speak. We are selective. We filter our intake from the real world through an intricate mesh of emotional and volitional experiences, prejudices and decisions. The ethicists' acknowledgment of unconscious motivation is a witness to the fact that the depths of the human heart cannot be sounded.

The subject of this book may itself serve as an illustration of the filtering process. Much has been written on discernment in the past few decades. A large percentage of this literature deals with processes and techniques, a subject hardly mentioned in Scripture. Little in the popular literature deals with the heart of the biblical doctrine of discernment: how and when God enlightens us, the conditions for receiving his light (it is not cheaply given), signs of the Spirit, inner and outer verification, implications for teachers in the Church. Discernment of God's mind can be learned only at the lips of the Lord. Yet most of what has been said derives from what men think.

As one travels about lecturing, he gets the feeling that many people are weary of hearing about discernment processes. These processes have not worked any better or worse than other approaches to problem solving, and so they are left aside as another mere fad. Speakers have been invited for "a weekend of discernment", and their audiences have probably felt that afterward they knew all about the subject even though most of the biblical message may not have been mentioned, let alone developed.

One brief example will make the point clear (chapter 6 will discuss it at length). God reveals *his* wisdom only to the humble (Ps 25:9). The Father shares his mysteries with the little ones, not with the conceited (Lk 10:21). I may use the most efficient discernment process in the world, but if I am vain, I will end up with nothing other than my "wisdom"—which St. Paul tells us is foolishness to God. If I am filled up with my own light, God does not force his into me.

Discernment processes are useful, but only after the biblical conditions and signs are operative. The processes may be 2 percent of the matter. This volume aims at dealing with the other 98 percent.

I hope it can be said modestly that no current work does what this volume attempts. A few competent but highly technical biblical studies have appeared (for example, Gerard Therrien's *Le Discernement dans les écrits pauliniens*, 1973), but even these tend to be limited in scope. The studies I have seen do not reckon sufficiently with many of the biblical themes that bear on getting to the divine mind even though they (the biblical themes) do not always use the few Greek discernment expressions. These Greek terms we shall consider in chapter 5, but we will deal also with related biblical streams of thought. Both together give a full picture of the scriptural doctrine on discerning the Spirit.

Does God speak to us today? If he does, who can know it? In our age of conflicting ideologies, where is the truth? In a Church beset with clashing theologies, who can detect the biblical "sound doctrine"? Who can know personally in his own heart that he himself is genuine? Partially? Fully? Is there any solid basis for supposing that eternal wisdom breaks through into our time-bound confusions? This volume will expand and explore these questions in part I. In part II it will investigate the possibility of discernment and the conditions that must be fulfilled for its achievement. Part III will discuss biblical signs and criteria indicating the presence of the Holy Spirit and a being led by him. Part IV will relate the inner elements of discernment to the outer structural "testing" of which the New Testament speaks. It will also apply the main message of the book to ethics and to current theological pluralism.

ACKNOWLEDGMENTS

Grateful acknowledgment is made to the editors of *Review for Religious* and *Spiritual Life* for the adapted use of one previously published article from each periodical. Likewise our final chapter contains sections from two articles that have appeared in the *Homiletic and Pastoral Review*. No little gratitude is due to Sister Mary Vincent Fritton, S.C.L., for her careful and competent reading of the completed manuscript of the first edition and for her helpful corrections and suggestions.

I should also like to express appreciation and thanks to Anne Nash for her admirable diligence and skill in editing the text of this new edition of *Authenticity*.

PART ONE

CONCEPTS AND PROBLEMS

I

ANATOMY OF AUTHENTICITY

The reader of these pages should be ready for surprises. God's mind is not our mind, his ways not our ways. What merely human wisdom says about all sorts of things, discernment of the Spirit included, is a long way off from what divine wisdom says. We shall pursue the latter while not neglecting the former.

This book is necessarily radical. It is radical for the simple reason that God is the Primordial Radical, the Unexpected. We tend to utter truisms about discernment. He will shake us to our roots. Years of working with Scripture have taught me that the most explosive divine concepts (for example, continual prayer, complete detachment, a sparing-sharing life-style), while they at first seem impossible, are seen upon further study to be absolutely correct. It is quite otherwise with human wisdom. At first it has the appearance of truth, but upon further testing and experience, it is found to be lacking in only too many cases.

In an age of mass media beautiful concepts are easily cheapened, even mauled. By overuse a magnificent idea can be trivialized. By abuse it can be degraded. An obvious example is the word *love*.

A less obvious example is the concept of discernment. Splendid in itself, it has become only too often a synonym for discussion, sometimes mingled with prayer, sometimes not. Popular literature and lectures have tended to present discernment largely as a process to be pursued either individually or in community. People commonly speak of a "weekend of discernment" or "discerning with my spiritual director or superior". All this can be good, of course, but it can also be simplistic. The New Testament says nothing about discernment processes but much about the conditions of detecting the mind of God. What has been said about our entering the deep silence of God is applicable to the core reality of discernment: "There are no techniques in spiritual life, except perhaps for the outer layers of it."[1] Most popular writings on our subject seem to be content with the outer layer. Some people are understandably weary with this literature because it looks like another fad, a fad that actually does not work much better than simple communal discussions. One may feel that somehow he has heard it all before.

Yet this is not the case. The most important elements in discerning the Holy Spirit are scarcely mentioned in the literature of the past few decades. These important elements are the subject of this book. We shall not repeat what has been amply said about processes and techniques. This we shall suppose. Our concern shall center on what is far more important.

Among things that are more important is a conversion readiness, for not all those who *think* they are listening to the Holy Spirit *are* listening to the Holy Spirit. This readiness implies so basic an inner change that we ought not

---

[1] Abhishiktananda, *Prayer* (ISPCK, 1967), p. 48.

easily to suppose we have achieved it. Scripture says a great deal about the conditions necessary before one is uncluttered enough to detect the gentle voice of God speaking in the depths of the person.

In one way discernment is most simple, that is, when one has become a saint. In another way it is complex, even impossible, that is, when one is a sinner. Because most of us would be inclined to select the latter category as self-descriptive, the message of this volume is necessary. It is not written for illuminists, those who have so assured themselves that they have a privileged access to the Holy Spirit that no amount of external evidence will change their mind. It is written for us publicans who know ourselves to be sinners and ignorant of many things. It is written for the little ones and the repentant, because it is to these that the Father has chosen to reveal his mysteries (Lk 10:21–22).

Discernment is no fad. It works. But only discernment according to the divine mind works. Anything less turns out to be another gimmick here today and gone tomorrow. The genuine article shares in the stability of its Author: Yesterday, today, yes, and forever.

A Contemporary Formulation

If one wishes a one-word summary of the biblical teaching on getting to the mind of God, the word is authenticity. After some years of studying discernment in Sacred Scripture, I slowly realized that the root of the whole matter is conversion, complete conversion. Why this is so will become progressively clear as we move along.

What is authenticity? Our English word derives from the Greek *authentikos*, primary or original. It refers to a correspondence to the factual situation, a not-being-false or merely an appearance. Authenticity is reality without sham. An ancient manuscript is said to be authentic when its origin is verified by adequate evidence, internal and external.

"Man tends by nature toward the truth" (CCC 2467). The human person is authentic to the extent that he lives the truth. He conforms his mind, words, actions to what is. His mind reflects reality, and his speech reflects his mind. Synonyms therefore are: honesty, fidelity, reliability, trustworthiness, genuineness.

But more is required. The human person must be whole to be completely authentic. In the present economy of salvation, wholeness demands divinization. There is only one enough for man, and that is the divine Enough. Anything less is incomplete, truncated. We are dynamically orientated to the absolute Holy One, to him who is fullness of beauty, truth, love, joy, ecstasy. There is consequently no fully authentic "natural man". The Father made us in the image of his Son, so that anything less than conformity to this image is a falling away from the *authentikos*, the original. "The disciple of Christ consents to 'live in the truth,' that is, in the simplicity of a life in conformity with the Lord's example, abiding in his truth" (CCC 2470).

The genuine man or woman measures up to the real, to the factual situation. He is humble because he knows and professes himself to be neither more nor less than he actually is. He is single-minded in his pursuits, for he operates with the pure motivation of eating and drinking and doing all else for the glory of God (1 Cor 10:31), a thing easy to say but impossible to do without its being a divine gift. He accepts the whole gospel, not simply the popular, pleasant parts of it. He welcomes correction because he knows himself to be ignorant of many things and a sinner besides (Prov 9:7–9). He is patient when suffering rejection for he knows that those who do live fully in conformity to Christ Jesus are sure to be persecuted (2 Tim 3:12). He is unafraid to speak out the truth, the unpopular truth (2 Cor 4:2). Especially is he authentic because he is a total lover of God, and love brings all the other ingredients of authenticity (1 Cor 13:4–7).

A Classical Formulation

Authenticity coincides with sanctity. The saint alone is fully real, honest, faithful, loving, genuine. He alone is immersed in beauty, truth, ecstasy. The classical, theological way of thinking about authenticity was to think of virtue, especially heroic virtue.

What is heroic virtue? It is goodness to a superlative degree, a degree that far surpasses the mere natural resources of the human person. Over the course of the centuries the Church developed a detailed theology of saintliness, a theology that included definite criteria for determining in canonization processes the eminent perfection to which God calls us (Mt 5:48). Heroic goodness is a specific human quality (humility, patience, purity, love) that shows itself in actions that are (1) promptly, easily, joyfully done; (2) even in difficult circumstances; (3) habitually, not just occasionally; (4) present actually, not just potentially; (5) found mingled with all the virtues.

A few examples will make the concept easy to grasp. A person possesses heroic humility when promptly and easily he avoids vanity in dress, domination in conversation, or desire to impress. He experiences little difficulty in accepting correction—indeed, he desires it. He is content and at peace with accusation, neglect, blame, rejection. He quite literally finds a joy in all this after the word of Jesus: "Happy are you when people abuse you and persecute you and speak all kinds of calumny against you on my account. Rejoice and be glad . . ." (Mt 5:11–12). This heroic humility is practiced even in difficult circumstances (for example, when one is alone without human support) and habitually, not just occasionally. It is not merely potential, a being able in one circumstance or another. Rather it is an actually lived reality. It is found with the totality of the virtues: patience, gentleness, frugality and all the others.

Another example: faith. Faith is heroic when one accepts God's revelation in Scripture and in the teaching of the Church not simply as a cultural heritage but because of his divine knowledge and truth. The acceptance is not selective but entire, and it is prompt, easy, joyful. One adheres to the divine self-disclosure not only when one's companions also adhere but even when, for example, the Church's teaching is widely rejected, when one may be persecuted for fidelity either psychologically and/or physically. The man of heroic faith stands by the biblical word and the teaching Church day by day, not only when he has the human support of his friends. Like Thomas More, he is ready to stand up to kings and bishops who reject the Holy See, and he is so joyful in his confession of truth that he may be able to joke, as Thomas did, with his executioners.

A third illustration: purity. The heroically chaste person is not the little boy or girl who has no idea of what impurity is all about, who has suffered no unchaste allurement or temptation. Rather, he is the person who even in the midst of sensual advertising and immodest dress readily and easily and joyfully resists the degradation and cheapening of the human body. This is the person who so reverences the divine gift of sexuality that he experiences no great problem in loving others in a pure delight. This chastity has nothing of rigidity or coldness about it but is easily warm, gentle, strong, joyous. Needless to say, it is rooted in a profound faith, hope, love, humility.

A fourth example: obedience. Heroic obedience is neither reluctant nor selective. One happily carries out all the directives of his superior because he sees the divine hand in them. The execution of a command is prompt, not delayed. The task is easily, joyfully done, habitually done. The obedient person makes it a joy for the superior to be in charge (Heb 13:17), and he obeys even when the director is unworthy to be in a leadership position (Mt 23:1–7). This submission is humble, gentle, trusting, loving.

A final example: patience. The average individual can on rare occasions bite his tongue in annoying circumstances and perhaps barely restrain a sharp word if not a disapproving glance. The heroically patient person is habitually calm in aggravating situations, and he readily, even joyfully, responds to the unkind remark or gaze or action. He knows how to turn the cheek, and he does it easily. He is joyful with those who rejoice and is sad with those in sorrow. He treats all, friends and enemies alike, with equal kindness (Rom 12:15–16) even though he may be closer to some persons than to others.

And so it goes with all the theological and moral virtues. It takes little imagination to see that the Church's age-old criteria for determining who is a saint and who is not are so many indicators of authenticity. The picture is demanding, but it is beautiful. A close analysis of St. John of the Cross' teaching on the transforming union discloses the almost incredible beauty of a person who has been transformed by an entire immersion in God. Advancing prayer brings about what St. Paul speaks of as a growth from one glory to another as we are transformed by the indwelling Spirit into his own image (2 Cor 3:18).

Ramifications of Authenticity

Most people want to be authentic, but few attain authenticity in any fullness. Even aside from the fact that no one of us can attain heroic holiness without a long process of gospel living, we often enough do not realize the thoroughgoing character of it and the ramifications that stem from it. We may therefore suggest how authenticity would apply to several areas of gospel living.

   1. *Spiritual direction.* While the message of Christ is proclaimed to the assembly, it must also be applied to the individual. Spiritual direction aims at detecting the action of the Holy Spirit in the unique person's efforts to live the precepts of the gospel. The spiritual director is precisely that, a director. He is not a superior, not primarily a teacher. He is a guide who helps a person discern the leading of the Spirit and through this leading achieve his own unique authenticity. We are, all of us, so prone to rationalizing away the requirements of the good news that we need the authoritative teaching of the Church, the guidance of leaders (business, civil, religious) and, in some cases, the direction of a man or woman of prayer.

   They are under no small illusion who consider that they may judge the official teachings of those Jesus has sent to speak in his name but who feel no need to be admonished by confessor or spiritual director. It is not surprising that those who do actually attain the authenticity of heroic virtue are the very ones most attached to the teaching Church and the guidance of her faithful priests. The catalogue of the saints is replete with examples. It goes without saying that competent spiritual direction is impossible without a knowledge of the biblical theology of discernment. People who give retreats or spiritual direction without this knowledge are treading where angels would fear to go.

2. *Growth in prayer.* St. John of the Cross once remarked that many who think their prayer life is almost nil are actually praying well, while others who consider their prayer to be flourishing are scarcely praying at all.[2] Experienced spiritual directors know that illusion in prayer development is not rare. Many people do not realize that prayer cannot be divorced from one's style of life. "Prayer and *Christian life* are *inseparable*, for they concern the same love and the same renunciation, proceeding from love" (CCC 2745). If one does not live gospel humility, detachment, love, obedience and all the rest, he cannot grow in prayer. He is not authentic. He is not listening to the Holy Spirit no matter how convinced he may be that the Spirit is speaking to him (and he is only too often unshakably so convinced). The signs of the Holy Spirit that we shall consider in later chapters are of no little worth in evaluating prayer development, one's own or another's.

3. *Liturgical vitality.* Inauthenticity often enough cloaks itself in external proprieties that cover over either emptiness or perversity. Even so sacred a reality as the liturgy is not exempt from the possibility of a pharisaical concern for visible practices devoid of inner devotion. A liturgical

[2] *Ascent of Mount Carmel*, prologue.

renewal that focuses on symbols, musical instruments, varied readings or colorful banners but shows little concern for the depth of inner prayer is subject to the biblical reproach against a people who paid the Lord God lip service and yet had a heart far from him (Is 29:13; Mk 7:6–7). Genuine liturgy is a worship of the Father in spirit and in truth (Jn 4:23). It is not a mere sham appearance, because it flows out of chaste hearts full of burning love for God. It is primary, original, faithful. It renews God's people and makes them into the new creation. It is the power center for the rest of the day: work, recreation, private prayer.

4. *Interpreting Scripture.* Just as God's word is both a divine and a human word, so understanding it is both a divine and a human task. The technician without a shred of faith can grasp ancient languages and profit from archeological finds, and thus he can attain to a certain knowledge of the biblical word. But it is like the knowledge of a person from a picture alone. The inner meaning and spirit are missing. A profound knowledge of Scripture is born only of deep inner communion with the indwelling Spirit who enlightens the inner eye. St. Teresa of Avila had no biblical degree, but there is no doubt she possessed an understanding of revelation simply unattainable by the scholar who is not also a mystic. The same is true of Augustine of Hippo, Catherine of Siena and the Curé of Ars. The man or woman of heroic sanctity enjoys an insight into divine revelation that is closed to the mere technician. To see our point, one need only read side by side a mediocre commentary together with St. Ambrose's commentary on Luke or St. Augustine's on John. The differences are like those between a picture and a person. Once again authenticity is wholeness. It is not a mere appearance or a shell.

5. *Giving advice.* Offering counsel to another is in itself a noble task, for in it one aids in shaping another life of inestimable value, a life for which Christ died. Yet this task, too, can be less than authentic. One can give advice with the more or less realized aim of forming the listener into one's own image. One can advise in order to impress or to dominate. That one may advise "in all wisdom" (Col 3:16), he needs to be himself formed into the gospel image through much prayer and pondering of the word. And, if the advice lies in a secular enterprise, he needs competency in that field. Aiding a person in discerning the Spirit is not simply a coming together with him in prayer and discussion. One is fit to advise to the extent that he is virtuous. Study and intellectual competence are important, of course, but in the ways of the Spirit a fullness of love has no substitute.

6. *Seeking advice.* We have noted that the human person is authentic to the extent that he lives the truth. He relates to others without sham. Part of living the truth is an acceptance of a reasonable dependence on others, an acknowledgment of a need for admonition and advice. But not any advice will do. There is the type of person who seeks advice (for example, in spiritual direction or in a directed retreat) but selects his adviser according to the type of counsel he wants to hear. One who has little inclination toward a frugal life-style is not likely to seek the counsel from one who is so inclined. This is not living the truth.

7. *Speech and silence.* From the abundance of the heart the mouth speaks (Lk 6:45). Sooner or later inner authenticity shows itself in outer words. The wisdom literature of the Old Testament abounds in advice on the use of speech. We read that the holy man speaks little, namely,

only when it is useful or necessary. He knows the opportune time for words and the opportune time for silence. When he does speak, he thinks first and carefully weighs what he shall say and how he shall say it. He is honest and simple. Although the signs of the Holy Spirit that we shall investigate later in this volume stem from inner integrity, their visible visage appears largely in speech, for it is in our conversation especially that we exteriorize our inner richness or poverty, our inner truth or sham.

8. *The wide vision.* Because authenticity implies wholeness, comprehensiveness, the genuine person manages to avoid the narrowness of partial positions. Most people tend to allow the truth they possess so to dominate their thinking that they see few other truths that place their one truth in perspective and balance it out. There is probably no heresy in the history of the Church that did not have its truth. The problem invariably is that the one truth so took over the heretic's mind that he was committed to cast out any number of other doctrines that clashed with his interpretation of it. The place of work and prayer in our lives may serve as an illustration. Few people are large-minded enough fully to accept in practice the teaching of Vatican Council II that we are to be "eager to act and devoted to contemplation" (SC no. 2). Most people are eager for one, not both of these (it may be granted that a few are eager for neither). This is one root reason there are so few fully authentic people in our world. Minds tend to be narrow, partial.

9. *Vocational fidelity.* Comprehensive large-mindedness eminently applies to one's view of his vocation and to the actual living out of it. The husband or wife who views marriage as a combination of single liberty and wedded fidelity appears to have a large mind, but it is actually nar-

row. It is not wide enough to embrace the wholeness of one vocation and to live it thoroughly. The narrowness is the smallness of self-centeredness. The religious who seeks the joys of two worlds and avoids the sacrifices of both of them is inauthentic. Simple, common people may not understand much of technical philosophy or theology, but they know well what is being said here.

Roots of Illusion

The very fact that a person picks up a book with the title of this one is an indication of a desire for authenticity. Yet in this matter desire is not the problem. Unwitting illusion is.

If illusion means unrealized, possibly sincere, even enthusiastic error, there is far more of it in each of our lives than we are prepared to admit. All the way from our petty vanities to suppositions about our motivations, we are subject to all sorts of misjudgments concerning the way things are. There are the illusions of exaggerated self-esteem and its opposite, a weak self-image. There are the hundreds of illusory desires of which St. Paul speaks (Eph 4:22), desires for things we imagine we need. There are our illusory fears of things we ought not at all to fear ("What will they think of me? How will I look?") and the illusory nonfear of things we ought dreadfully to fear. There are the many misjudgments of what is important in life and what is trivial—and who, if he be less than a saint, does not err in these judgments dozens of times each day? Then there are the more gross illusions of those who are convinced that they are listening to God himself even though all the signs point in the opposite direction?

If human powers for knowing are made for contact with the real world, for the attainment of truth, how is illusion possible? If our senses and intellects are essentially healthy and therefore capable of truth, why do we slip into error? If a normal eye cannot see what is not before it, why are there optical illusions? If a normal mind cannot know what is not, why does it make judgments about what is not?

To explain error and illusion by the simple expedient of saying that our knowing powers are faulty may be convenient, but it is not true. The roots of illusion lie much deeper, in the center of the human person. We may not like to admit it, but careful analysis shows that we err basically because of a defect in free choice. This defect is not always obvious and blatant. Often it is not realized. But it is still present. Error stems fundamentally from sin, at least objective sin that traces its root ultimately to subjective sin. How do we explain this?

Error properly speaking is found, not in a mere perception, but in a judgment, in an affirmation or a denial. If I see a fruit tree in the distance with small, round, red objects hanging from the branches, I have not yet fallen into any error. I see what I see. If, however, I affirm "those are apples", when as a matter of fact they are plums, my judgment is an erroneous judgment. I am now in error, under illusion. Why did this happen when my eyes perceived correctly what was in front of them?

It did not happen necessarily. I did not have to affirm that the small red objects were apples. I could have freely withheld judgment and more sensibly said that they might be apples or some similar looking fruit. When I see a stick apparently bent in the water, I do not have to say it is bent. I could affirm only what my eyes actually do see: apparent bending. The error is not in what my eyes perceive; it is in what my intellect judges.

Philosophers have long noted that error proximately is due to an extension of one's judgment beyond evidence. For an ancient to have affirmed that the earth is flat was no fault in vision. It was extending judgment beyond available evidence. We moderns do the same thing every day. Someone on the street mistakes one person at some distance for another simply by unwittingly stretching a mere similarity into an identity. Doctors only too often diagnose illnesses without sufficient evidence for an apodictic judgment. People make mistaken judgments about the morality of contraception or abortion without anything resembling adequate study or evidence. Religious say things about the meaning of their life that no evidence from revelation supports.

Yet we have not yet reached the root of error. Why do we so commonly extend our affirmations and denials beyond sufficient foundation? There are a number of immediate causes. At one time we do it because of haste. We are too slothful to study the matter carefully. Or we may be hasty because we wish to impress others with our rapid answer or keen insight. At another time the immediate problem is vanity. We do not wish to admit ignorance, and so we make a judgment even though sufficient support is lacking. At still another time we err because we like a position, not because it is well supported. Pleasure, fashion, life-style and conformism are mighty causes of error. Many people accept moral norms, not because they have carefully thought them out, but because these norms are easy and "everybody is doing it."

Another common reason we extend our judgments beyond evidence is an emotional pressure of one type or

another. Fear, joy, anguish, elation, anger obviously inter-
fere with cool reasoning and therefore with insight. These
same emotions prompt one to think and say things for
which he has no intellectual grounds.

We still have not reached the deepest source of error.
Why do we utter the mistaken judgment through sloth or
vanity or attachment or conformism or emotion? We do
not have to do it. The deepest source of error is the will.
We more or less knowingly choose to extend our judgment beyond solid evidence. Sometimes a person is so habitually under illusion that he has almost no awareness
that he has no basis for his position. His pleasures, con-
formisms, biases and vanities are so much part of his person that he has lost a critical capacity in their regard.

We err because we lack love. (I am not thinking here of
the surface, factual errors children are taught by mis-
education or inexperienced adults through propaganda.)
There are such things as volitional impingements on insight. Defective motivation induces intellectual darkness.
The more one loves, the more he sees ultimate reality.
Love puts one into contact with God and with men as
nothing else does. The person who loves fully sees deeply.

He sees deeply because he is free of the thousand emotional and willed obstructions to inner vision. He feels no
need to feign knowledge when he is ignorant. His passions
do not prompt him to embrace an illusory but lax morality. Just as there is no one so blind as he who wills not to
see, so there is no one so seeing as he who wills to love. He
is authentic.

2

THE PROBLEMS OF DISCERNMENT

As the academic world of ideas has lived its life through the centuries, its progress has been flawed far more frequently by negations than by affirmations. Most of what we affirm is correct. When we go astray, the problem is usually found in what we do not affirm. Either we fail to put our truth into its context, or we fail to condition it with other equally important truths, or we exaggerate it beyond the limits of reality.

Just as this is true in our individual lives, so it is true in public life, secular and religious. In the latter we are safe in saying that most aberrations have enclosed a kernel of truth. The Montanists, the Waldenses, the Brothers of the Free Spirit, the Alumbrados, the Jansenists all had a hold on truth. Their aberrations began at precisely the point where they rejected or neglected other truths.

We are happily experiencing a renewed interest in the discernment of spirits. The charismatic, prophetic aspects of the gospel were allowed in the past too easily to fall into the shade. Much of what has been written in recent years is worthwhile. Yet there are more than a few omissions. There is a great deal more to the discernment of spirits than many of us realize. In this chapter we shall consider some of the problems that must be faced and some of the questions that are begging for answers.

Two problems I shall leave aside. One is too obvious, the other too abstruse. The first is authoritarianism, quenching the Spirit, the old rigorism that did much deciding but little listening. This problem has lessened, but it is still found in the Church, sometimes in unexpected places. In any event it has been talked to death. The second problem is the theoretical possibility of divine revelation: Can God reveal himself publicly and/or privately? Is the chasm between finite and infinite so vast that it is unbridgeable? I shall assume as shown elsewhere that the answer to the first question is affirmative, to the second, negative.

The Problem of Terminology

The many people who use the term "discernment" do not necessarily use it in the same sense. In the more popular mind, it is a synonym for prayerful inquiry or communal discussion. When we turn to the technical literature, we find a number of significantly different concepts. St. Thomas considered that the *"discretio spirituum"* referred usually to an extraordinary gift of knowing future happenings or to a reading of the secrets of hearts.[1] The saint seldom spoke of our simple *discretio* but considered it part of prudence.[2] St. John of the Cross looked upon discernment to be a sure, infused, deeply embedded knowledge of finite things, deeds, events.[3] Cardinal Bona (died 1674) wrote of

---

[1] I-II, q. 111, a. 4.

[2] Joseph Pegon, "Discernment of Spirits", NCE 4:894.

[3] *Ascent of Mount Carmel*, bk. 2, chap. 26, no. 11; Kieran Kavanaugh and Otilio Rodriguez, eds., *The Collected Works of St. John of the Cross* (Washington, D.C.: ICS, 1979), p. 196. Our citations of John will be taken from this translation.

an effort "to detect among various motions whether one inclination comes from the good or the bad spirit, whether this be in the area of morals or doctrine".[4] In our own day John J. O'Rourke considers discernment of spirits to be "the ability to discern the origin of extraordinary phenomena".[5] He is commenting on 1 Corinthians 12:10. K. A. Wall refers to discernment as a penetrating perception into spiritual matters and the spiritual condition of persons.[6] John Futrell defines our subject as a "sifting through of interior experiences in order to determine their origin and to discover which ones are movements toward following the way of light."[7] Edward Malatesta speaks of "the process by which we examine, in the light of faith and in the connaturality of love, the nature of the spiritual states we experience in ourselves and in others".[8] Edward O'Connor remarks that discernment of spirits "has to do with determining whether the inspirations or impulses that come into our minds originate from God, Satan, or ourselves".[9] Alois Stoger, in commenting on 2 Peter 2:1, speaks of God permitting "false prophets in his church to test his people on their undivided love of him and their ability to distinguish between truth and error".[10] J. Pegon writes that "the proper act of discernment con-

[4] Jacques Guillet et al., *Discernment of Spirits* (Collegeville, Minn.: Liturgical Press, 1970), p. 92.

[5] John J. O'Rourke, in *A New Catholic Commentary on Holy Scripture* (Nashville: Nelson, 1975), p. 1156.

[6] K. A. Wall, "Direction, Spiritual", NCE 4:887.

[7] John Futrell, *Ignatian Discernment* (St. Louis, Mo.: American Assistancy Seminar on Jesuit Spirituality, 1970), pp. 47–48.

[8] Edward Malatesta, in Guillet et al., *Discernment*, p. 9.

[9] Edward O'Connor, *Pastoral Newsletter*, May 1971, p. 5.

[10] Alois Stoger, *The Second Epistle of Peter*, in *New Testament for Spiritual Reading* (hereafter: NTSR), vol. 22 (London: Burns and Oates, 1969), p. 156.

sists less in judging the origin of these phenomena (e.g., illuminations, inspirations, consolations, dryness, visions, messages) than in recognizing their orientation." [11]

The differences among these concepts of discernment are not in every case trivial, and yet there are interrelations and overlapping. If we consider the biblical account as a whole, it seems that discernment includes both detecting the origin of our inclinations, desires, inspirations and insights and evaluating the signs by which one might know if a given course of action or teaching seems to be of God or not. The two meanings are closely intertwined.

The Problem of Subjective Illusion

Those who have the most reliable experience of God place the least stock in it. Those who readily speak of listening to the Spirit for specific directions are probably the least likely to be in contact with him. In the whole of the Church's history, our most authentic and lofty mystics are the men and women who are the least impressed with detailed messages from God. If those holding that position were religious sceptics, we would have no problem. We could merely say that the latter did not believe in the Holy Spirit's operation and our experience of him. But the mystics believe profoundly in both. Yet they brush divine communications aside as though they were of small importance. Even more, they look on "contact with God" as extremely open to illusion. What are we to think, then, of the many others who speak easily of listening to the Spirit, who define obedience as an immediate awareness of God and his will?

[11] Pegon, "Discernment", 4:894.

Today we would add to this what ethicists commonly point out, namely, that all of us are much affected by unconscious motivation. We may be able to articulate some of the reasons we do what we do, but there are assuredly other motivations of which we are unaware. I like to flatter myself into believing that my positions in matters political and moral are the results of clear, cool thought processes. They may be to some extent, hopefully, but they are also the results of my early experiences, my tastes, my free choices and my life-style. Even aside from the influence of the Holy Spirit, we can be subject to no little amount of illusion as to the real mainsprings of our inspirations and actions and statements. People who speak facilely of listening to the Spirit have little comprehension of human nature, let alone passively received experiences of God.

Purification and the Possibility of Discernment

If God teaches the humble his way (Ps 25:4–5, 9), opens the eyes of our mind (Ps 119:18), enlightens us from within our being (Jn 14:15–17, 26), fills us with insight (Eph 1:17) and wisdom (James 1:5) and gives our very desires and decisions (Phil 2:13), we must ask how a reasonably sincere person could possibly fail to detect his workings. Yet this truth must be combined with another: Those in our history who have been most marvelously enlightened by the Holy Spirit are the least inclined to consider this enlightenment easy to come by.

Whatever the explanation, it is bad methodology, when we have two well-established truths that appear to clash, to deny one of them. This solution is simple and pat, and it may appear expedient, but it is also false. How, then, do we reconcile these two well-founded propositions: (1) God does enlighten from within; and (2) many people who think they have detected his workings actually have not?

We can find a clue in this problem in an explanation given by St. John of the Cross as to why divine light does not illumine immediately but only after a while. Although God does cast light into our hearts from the beginning, we do not perceive it because it first illumines what is nearest to us, our failings and sins. This we find painful, dark, difficult. But after the divine light and love have burned away our sinfulness, we then begin more and more to be capable of perceiving the positive goods God is giving.[12] At the outset our knowing capacities are simply unable to perceive in a lofty, divine manner but only in their crude, human way. After the purifications of the dark nights of sense and spirit, our minds and desires are "prepared for the sublime reception, experience, and savor of the divine and supernatural, which is unreceivable until the old man dies".[13] This is one reason St. Paul teaches that only the mature can discern the Spirit—only they are pure enough to detect his light, his mind.

Though this goes a long way in solving one question, it raises some others. If the reception of divine illumination requires a purified person, is it realistic to speak of discerning sessions as though we can turn them off and on at will? Is not a "weekend of discernment" possibly simplistic? Do we consider sufficiently whether the profound conversion that must go on in each heart before discernment, individual or communal, is even possible? Do we see that prayer within the discerning process is far more than min-

---

[12] *Dark Night of the Soul*, bk. 2, chap. 13, no. 10; p. 360.
[13] Ibid., chap. 16, no. 4; p. 364.

gling reflection with dialogue? Do we suspect that perfect discernment is possible only when it is accompanied by a lofty, dark contemplation?

Problems of Interpretation

We may suppose now that one sensitive to the inner movements of the Holy Spirit is advancing both in his purification and in his contemplation. Our next query bears on the interpretation of the divine communication. Even when one does receive a valid inspiration from God, it is still possible to misunderstand or misapply it. There is evidence that the saints themselves have sometimes unwittingly mixed historical and theological errors into their visions. P. de Letter notes about the commonly admitted errors found even in authentic visionaries that there are particulars of time and place that have been added to the message. He notes that these people "are generally unable to make a distinction between the divine and the human elements".[14] If this can happen with honest, sincere, psychologically healthy people, namely, if one can mix his own limitations and error into the divine inspiration, can the theory and practice of discernment be content with private interpretation?

---

[14] P. de Letter, "Revelations, Private", NCE 12:446–47. St. John of the Cross explains that part of this distortion is due to the human intellect not being fully illumined by God and thus mixing in some of its own ideas and conclusions. Thus it will "immediately baptize all as coming from God and with such a supposition say, 'God told me,' 'God answered me.' Yet such is not so, but, as we pointed out, these persons themselves are more often the origin of their locution" (*Ascent of Mt. Carmel*, bk. 2, chap. 29, nos. 3–4; p. 204).

Problem of Spirit–Structure Tensions

If it is possible that experience of the divine be either valid or invalid, genuine or illusory, and if, moreover, even an authentic experience may be interpreted rightly or wrongly, accurately or inaccurately, the problem of criteria by which to judge experiences inevitably arises.

When one gets down deep below the surface in the discussion of religious differences, he will find that at the very bottom of other more or less important differences there lies a fundamental diversity. One type of person appeals to experience as the ultimate criterion by which he decides what is religiously relevant, while another type appeals to an external authority. Even persons who appeal to Scripture as an external authority finally come to the point where they part company. And they part ultimately because one values his own interpretation as the final criterion, while the other values the interpretation of his ecclesial community.

Religious experience as the final criterion of truth is, of course, the Protestant position. W. J. Hill was able to say that religious experience assumed its predominant role in Christianity only with the advent of the reformers in the sixteenth century. "In the 4 centuries from Luther to William James," he notes, "there is one common note in all of Western Christianity aside from Catholicism, namely, that religious experience is the ultimate criterion and rule of faith. Every constraint of dogma, authority, and speculative reason is to give way to it."[15] Thus a theology of discernment has deep ecclesiological roots. We find already in the New Testament a strong insistence on the subjec-

---

[15] W. J. Hill, "Experience, Religious", NCE 5:752.

tive being regulated by the objective, the experiential being tested and guided by the institutional. Contemporary
Scripture commentators routinely bring this out in their
exegesis. Bruce Vawter, for example, referring to the concern of 1 John that the faithful be protected from erroneous doctrine, remarks that "the safeguard of the true
Christian who would avoid the dire consequences of this
false teaching is to hold firmly to the teaching received
through the apostolic preaching." [16] Discussing Mark 6:11,
Rudolf Schnackenburg comments that "he who does not
receive the messengers of God excludes himself from salvation, faces the judgment of God, and is convicted by his
witnesses. As a sign that the messengers have nothing in
common with such places they are to shake even the dust
off their feet." [17] We have in 1 Corinthians 14:36–40 one of
the most pointed of texts dealing with the Spirit-structure
tension: private individuals are contesting the decisions of
authority. In the very chapter 14 that is so given to the
charismatic elements in the Corinthian church, Paul em-
phatically insists that the faithful obey his decision. If they
do not, they are not of the Spirit:

> Paul has now surely said the last word on this point. One
> feels in his sentences how great was the inclination of the
> Corinthians to judge everything from their own point of
> view and to question everything again and again. Against this
> Paul established decisively that no one is a Christian for him-
> self alone, so that he has only to judge according to his own
> insight. Being a Christian is only possible as a member of
> Christ's body and therefore by integration and subordina-
> tion. It may be that "in itself" there is always something
> more that could be said against it, but this cannot come from

[16] Bruce Vawter, in JBC 62:17.
[17] Rudolf Schnackenburg, *The Gospel according to St. Mark*, NTSR 3–4
(London: Sheed and Ward, 1971), 1:63–64.

a good spirit. . . . The man who is not willing to recognize it is not recognized by God.[18]

One final example illustrates how in the divine plan the inner impulse of the Spirit directs one to seek outer confirmation. Gerhard Schneider notes how Paul in Galatians 2:2f. undertakes the journey to Jerusalem, not on his initiative, but on God's: "A divine directive has impelled him to have his gospel ratified by the primitive community. . . . The decision can only be given by the 'men of repute.' He means the apostles," says Schneider, "who are the authorities in the community. God refers him to them, not them to him."[19]

Several questions therefore arise. Do contemporary discussions of discernment wrestle sufficiently with the ecclesial texts bearing on the subject? Should officeholders themselves be better instructed regarding discernment in general and their own testing functions in

---

[18] Eugen Walter, *The First Epistle to the Corinthians*, NTSR 13 (New York: Herder and Herder, 1971), pp. 154–55.

[19] Gerhard Schneider, *The Epistle to the Galatians*, NTSR 15 (London: Burns and Oates, 1969), p. 29. For further examples of similar exegesis, see Joseph A. Fitzmyer on Acts 20:29 and Galatians 1:6, in JBC 45:96 and 49:11; Alois Stoger, *The Gospel according to St. Luke*, NTSR 5–6 (London: Burns and Oates, 1969), 1:198; Henry Wansbrough, in *New Catholic Commentary*, p. 1079; Josef Kurzinger, *The Acts of the Apostles*, NTSR 10–11 (London: Burns and Oates, 1969–71), 2:101; Max Zerwick, *The Epistle to the Ephesians*, NTSR 16 (London: Burns and Oates, 1969), pp. 109–10; Franz Mussner, *The Epistle to the Colossians*, NTSR 17 (London: Sheed and Ward, 1971), p. 134; Joseph Reuss, *The Epistle to Titus*, NTSR 20 (London: Sheed and Ward, 1971), pp. 18–20, 42–43; Benedikt Schwank, *The First Epistle of Peter*, NTSR 21 (London: Burns and Oates, 1969), p. 44; John L. McKenzie, *Dictionary of the Bible* (New York: Macmillan Pub. Co., and London: Collier Macmillan, 1965), pp. 134, 136, 385, 413; André Barucq and Pierre Grelot, in DBT, p. 521; André Lemaire, *Biblical Theology Bulletin*, June 1973, p. 156; F. W. Young, *Interpreter's Dictionary of the Bible* (New York: Abingdon Press, 1962), 3:580–81; Augustin George and Pierre Grelot, in DBT 57.

particular? How do we persuade people to accept being tested? What is a quenching of the Spirit? How do we safeguard against it?

Factions as Impeding Communal Discernment

In our day we are so accustomed to disagreements, divisions and polarizations that we find it difficult to understand the remarkable insistence of the New Testament on *perfect* unity in community (Jn 17:23), on having oneness of mind (1 Cor 1:10; Phil 2:1–2), on agreement regarding doctrine (Acts 2:42; 4:32). We do not easily take to the idea that a household split into factions cannot endure for long (Mt 12:25). Especially we do not understand the Pauline idea that a community that is split into diverse ideologies is immature. The members, or at least some of them, are not living the gospel, are not led by the Holy Spirit. The apostle argues that he knows the Corinthians are worldly because they are divided (1 Cor 3:1–3). Division is a proof of communal immaturity, for the Spirit brings peace and harmony (Gal 5:22), whereas worldliness brings factions and dissensions (Gal 5:19). Basic divisions in a community pose three important problems for communal discernment.

If a divided community does not possess the Spirit insofar as it is divided, how can it possibly detect his mind?

If co-action follows on co-seeing (as it surely does), factions cannot produce anything coherent and unified and clear. They can produce only generalizations that promote individual projects. How then can a group describe itself and its way of life? How can a religious congregation hold a chapter in which the net result will not be vague, least-common-denominator generalizations?

Enlightened decision-making requires criteria by which proposals are evaluated. A divided group lacks these criteria because it has no shared vision. How then can it detect the finger of the Spirit?

What Is the Peace-Joy Experience?

Although peace as a sign of the Spirit's presence is one of the areas most talked about in discernment literature, a number of questions remain to be asked. Is this peace experience acquired by human endeavor alone, or is it also an infused gift of the Spirit? Is it only the latter? If it is humanly acquired, how is it a sign of the Holy Spirit? If it is given by him through what we commonly call infused contemplation, would it not follow that many persons could not claim peace as a sign of their discernment?

What is this peace-joy like from the experiential point of view? How does it differ from a mere emotional feeling of well-being or from the satisfaction one experiences when he gets his way?

Does peace as a sign of communal discernment require a unanimous acceptance of the group's decision? Why?

What is the communal peace experience? It cannot be merely an absence of overt conflict. It cannot be only a sense of freedom at the removal of restrictions. It cannot be the mere consequence of coming to the least common denominator after the group cannot agree on a specific solution. None of this is worthy of the Holy Spirit. A community must face particulars, and the Holy Spirit is calling it to specific decisions. Life cannot be lived in general. A failure to come to concrete solutions is probably due to members in the group blocking the influence of the Spirit through selfish clinging.

The Problem of Illuminism

At the outset of this chapter I suggested that errors commonly begin with a truth, but as they go their way they are seen in isolation from other truths that condition them, that give them a realistic context and orientation, that keep them healthy and sane. Every so often in the course of history we find the peculiar aberration called illuminism.

As its name suggests, illuminism is a doctrine (and even more, a practice) of the inner light. It is a truth gone wild, just as authoritarianism is an opposite truth gone wild. True to form, illuminism is rooted in the profound truth that God does enlighten every man who comes into this world (Jn 1:9). It accepts that the Holy Spirit of truth teaches us from within (Jn 14:15–17, 26; 16:13) and that if a man keeps the word of God, the Son manifests himself to him (Jn 14:21). Illuminists gladly embrace Paul's teaching that the Father radiates the light of his glory in our hearts (2 Cor 4:6) and gives us from within the very desires and decisions by which we serve him (Phil 2:13).

So far, so good. All this is true. But the historical problem with illuminism is that it knows only the inner light. It loses sight of or rejects another whole series of biblical texts (we have mentioned a fraction of them in preceding pages) that require guidance from an outer structure. The illuminist is so convinced of his inner light that no one either in civil society or in the hierarchical Church may admonish him or regulate his activity. Objective evidence brought against his position leaves not a dent in his subjective persuasion. His privileged inner source of light, his direct illumination by the Holy Spirit renders unnecessary the intervention of other human persons.

The illuminist is often an enthusiast, a person who deemphasizes the intellectual, objective approach and favors instead the avenue of subjective and direct access to God. Because he cuts himself off from the roots of his intellectual past and present, he easily gets attention. Ronald Knox has shrewdly observed that "the enthusiast, because he exaggerates, always has our sympathies in a given encounter. He cuts a finer figure, doing nothing by halves."[20] He need not be careful about distinctions and definitions. He need not mention conditioning elements in a problem. He can say things in a sweeping manner. And so the unwary and the slow-witted find him attractive. It can surprise one how easily he gathers a following.

Illuminism is a deadly enemy of discernment. One reason is that it invites an extreme reaction: the quenching of the Spirit by a new authoritarianism. Extremes beget one another. Antinomianism begets authoritarianism and vice versa. Another reason is that illuminism discredits discernment in the minds of the less informed. The genuine inner light is rejected because of the exaggerated inner light. A third reason is that illuminism naturally enough engenders rival illuminist camps. Says Knox:

> The pattern is always repeating itself, not in outline merely but in detail. Almost always the enthusiastic movement is denounced as an innovation, yet claims to be preserving, or to be restoring the primitive discipline of the Church. Almost always the opposition is twofold: good Christian people who do not relish eccentric spirituality find themselves in unwelcome alliance with worldlings who do not relish any spirituality at all. Almost always schism begets schism; once the instinct of discipline is lost, the movement breeds rival prophets and rival coteries, at the peril of its internal unity.

[20] Ronald Knox, *Enthusiasm*, p. 581.

Always the first fervours evaporate; prophecy dies out, and the charismatic is merged into the institutional.[21]

If, therefore, discernment of the Spirit is to have a fruitful future among us, we need to distinguish it clearly from illuminism both in theory and in practice. Those of us who speak and write about it would do well to study the history of illuminist movements all the way from Montanism to Jansenism right on into our own century.

Some Briefly Expressed Problems

Research into Scripture has indicated to me that there are approximately fifty themes (not texts merely, but themes) that bear on detecting the Spirit in our Christic economy. This revelation is so rich that even our remaining queries do not adequately excite our need for further study. Nonetheless, a few follow.

What are the "spirits" we have in mind when we speak in the plural? The Hebrew *ruah* and the Greek *pneuma* have a wide spectrum of related but diverse meanings. What do we mean when we speak of discerning the spirits?

God's thoughts are not our thoughts, and his ways are not our ways. If divine judgments are unexpected, extremely different from ours, how do we really listen to *him* speaking in human events? What is reading the signs of the times? How does this differ from a slavish conformism? This problem is so far from simple that those who think it easy of solution probably do not see the problem.

If, as Scripture repeatedly says, our sinfulness, our darkness, is the deep root of our errors in matters religious (for

[21] Ibid.

example, Jn 3:19; 7:33–34; 2 Th 2:10–11), conversion of the heart becomes an indispensable condition for even being capable of discerning the Holy Spirit. Does this not contradict our easy assumption that we *can* discern him? And if this is true, does it not follow that discernment is a far longer process than many of us imagine?

Scripture distinguishes the true from the false prophet. What are the signs that the divine word offers to the faithful that they may know the one from the other?

Detachment, inner freedom, absence of illusory desires are a condition for detecting the gentle inspirations of the Spirit of Jesus. Anyone who clings to a finite reality for its own sake is not clinging for God's sake, and thus he is blocking the illumination that comes from him. Any desire that stops in a finite reality is stopping short. It is like a cataract covering one's sight.[22] One is simply unable to grasp the higher wisdom of the Father of lights. When, we must then ask, is one detached? How is this detachment reconcilable with an appreciation for creation? Can one know if he is detached? How would we incorporate a theology of detachment into a theology of discernment?

This chapter suggests that discernment is a complex matter. Yet it must also be simple, since St. Paul supposes that ordinary people may attain a perfect knowledge and wisdom and understanding (Col 1:9). A Curé of Ars undoubtedly could detect the Spirit far better than a learned but unloving theologian. How then is discernment simple?

Among the biblical signs that characterize those who are led by the Spirit, those to whom the Father reveals his mysteries, we find humility, love, obedience. If, as St. Paul

---

[22] St. John of the Cross, *Living Flame of Love*, st. 3, no. 73; p. 639.

indicates, only the spiritually mature can detect the mind of God perfectly, ought we not to spend more energy in growing in humility, love and obedience? Techniques are undoubtedly useful in some situations, but without gospel holiness of life, they remain sterile.

A word must be added about discernment in spiritual direction. St. Teresa of Avila complained four centuries ago of the dearth of competent spiritual guides, and if one may judge from the commonness of current complaints, the situation is not changed today. St. John of the Cross, usually so gentle, has hard words for the blundering director who does not understand the delicate and sublime workings of the Holy Spirit in advancing persons. With these people there is at stake, he says, "almost an infinite gain in being right and almost an infinite loss in being wrong".[23] If the saint is right, can we easily suppose that almost anyone may rightly aid another in the attempt at discernment?

[23] Ibid., no. 56; p. 632.

3

HOW DOES GOD SPEAK?

Speak, Lord, for your servant is listening.—1 Kings 3:10

One need not emphasize that a vibrant sector of Christian life at this point in history is the sector of the Spirit, the Holy Spirit. The charismatic renewal has been promoting with no little success a whole life-style patterned on and growing out of a program centered in the Spirit's activity in the midst of God's people. This renewal is by no means restricted to "the release of the Spirit" or the gift of tongues or the healing ministry. It is felt that the Holy Spirit is speaking today not only to saints but to sinners, not only to officialdom but also to the lowly placed.

To some considerable extent, but not in an entire coincidence with the charismatic movement, the Spirit movement has been prominent in renewal efforts carried on in parishes and in religious life. Books, articles, lectures, chapter documents often refer to the Holy Spirit, especially under the rubric of openness to him, listening to him. The central thrust here is not so much prayer experience, speaking in tongues or engaging in a healing ministry as it is in detecting what God is saying to us, both to the individual and to the community.

This thrust toward listening to the Spirit is readily noted in the popularity of discernment methods, techniques and processes. The reality is surely of significance in an age struggling to find the mind of God and to read the signs of the times. If God does speak to his people—and Scripture insists that he does—it can never be unimportant to listen.

An Anomalous Situation

But this "listening" is where our problems begin, problems that press for solution. Before we can intelligently explain how one listens to the indwelling God, we should first understand something of how he speaks. The literature of our day, issuing both from the charismatic renewal and from religious-life circles, says almost nothing on this subject. As a matter of fact, I must candidly add that while speculative theologians often refer to the activity of the Holy Spirit in the Church, they seldom discuss how he acts and enlightens the individual through a personal contact. They do, of course, rightly point out that God speaks to his people through Scripture and through the representatives he has established in his Church: "He who hears you, hears me" (Lk 10:16).[1] But this is not the question at hand. People have in mind a personal, individual and/or communal encounter with the Holy Spirit, and in this encounter they feel they "listen to him".

Our situation, therefore, is odd. On the one hand, many people routinely speaking of "listening to the Spirit", as though he were as familiar as a friend speaking over their shoulder. Yet, on the other hand, almost no one explains how he speaks, even though we all know that he does not use sound waves. Nor are we told how one can be

[1] See also Jn 13:20; Jn 21:15–17; Lk 22:31–32; Titus 1:7; 1 Tim 3:15; 2 Tim 3:14–16 and many other like texts.

so sure it is the Spirit speaking. Until we provide satisfactory answers to the question "How does the Spirit speak?", we are left with some embarrassing problems. How can anyone be so sure he is listening to the Spirit and not to his own ideas and desires? We hardly need to debate the observation of Aldous Huxley: "The untutored egoist merely wants what he wants. Give him a religious education, and it becomes obvious to him, it becomes axiomatic, that what *he* wants is what God wants." [2] Does God speak in diverse ways? If he does, how can we know the differences? What are we to think of serious and sincere people who are convinced that they are receiving special messages from the Holy Spirit? Is good will enough to insure this kind of encounter with God?

Who Can Answer Our Questions?

If it is true that the popular and theological literature on the contemporary scene seldom discusses the title question of this chapter, one may rightly wonder who can answer it? I know of two sources: Scripture and the mystics. [3] We may acknowledge at the outset that the Lord God did speak to select representatives in biblical times and in extraordinary ways (Heb 1:1). However, we shall not be primarily concerned here with the divine messages addressed to public personages, to a Moses or to a Paul. Rather we shall direct our attention to the usual, frequent, routine ways God speaks to the inner heart of anyone close to him.

---

[2] *The Devils of Loudun*, p. 18.

[3] By "mystics" here, I do not refer to the recipients of extraordinary phenomena such as levitation or the stigmata. The word in Catholic theology indicates those men and women who have a deep experiential encounter with God.

The expression "experience of God" calls forth diverse reactions in diverse people. For some, mostly in the past, the word conjured up was illusion. For others, mostly in the present, the word speaks of encounter and answer. Oddly enough, both groups are right and wrong.

Because discerning the Spirit obviously implies an experience of him and his light, we must analyze with some adequacy what we mean by the expression and what problems it occasions. Too many discussions of discernment have conveniently bypassed this troublesome area. They speak of the peace experience, of listening to the Spirit, as though it were all immediately clear what is genuine and what is not.

What Is Experience?

Some realities we all know but can scarcely explain: being, time, spirit, matter. Experience is another. It is so general and pervasive that it is difficult to specify what the idea means. Yet we can explain something of it. Experience bespeaks an awareness caused by a presence, a contact with things inner or outer. The thing may be an outer object, a tree, or it may be nothing other than one's inner feeling of well-being or illness. One cannot experience tapioca (as distinguished from thinking about or recalling tapioca) unless he is influenced by its presence. Experience implies a passivity with a vital response. It is both cognitive and affective, with the latter predominating: pleasant-painful, hard-soft, warm-cold, clear-dull. Though one may choose some experiences, there is an element in experience that is unchosen, something beyond our control.[4] More briefly,

[4] Karl Rahner and Herbert Vorgrimler, *Theological Dictionary* (New York: Herder and Herder, 1965), p. 162.

we may say that experience is a received awareness of presence or the in-living of an object.

What Is the Experience of God?

When there is question of contacting God, we may speak of an experience continuum, a spectrum from weak to strong. On the weak side, we may possibly speak of experiencing God in music, poetry, artistic and natural beauty. Farther along one could mention the philosophical, deductive proofs for God's existence as modes of contacting him—although the passivity element in experience is by no means prominent. Transcendental Thomists note a still stronger encounter in free choice, especially in the embracing of absolute duty. They see a contact with God here because when one acts because of absolute goodness, he bursts beyond the realm of the finite into that of the infinite. Moving toward the strong side of the spectrum, we meet the mystical gift of advanced prayer, itself embracing a spectrum from delicate to strong. Finally, the most intense experience of God open to human persons is the direct encounter of beatific vision. This last, of course, being our final fulfillment, does not concern us in our discussion of discernment in pilgrimage.

Only the spiritually mature, the fully purified and converted are able to discern fully. St. Paul is lucid on this point. It is advancing prayer that brings about both the necessary purification and the intimacy of contact without which talk about discernment is mere chatter.

Whence Arises This Experience of God?

We have noted that experience in general implies a prior passivity and only then entails a living response. God originates the experience of God, no one else. The mystics are of one mind in their insistence that man is completely unable to initiate, continue or intensify the divine communication.[5] Contemplative prayer . . . "is a *gift*, a grace; it can be accepted only in humility and poverty" (CCC 2713). This point is important because there are people who speak too facilely of listening to God when there is no reason to think that they are tuned into anything more than some created reality or to their own human perception. "Some people today", notes Piet Fransen, "seem to be ready to speak of revelation as soon as they meet some kind of human spontaneity, new insight or creativity either poetical, artistical or philosophical. As long as this process remains a purely human, and thus a purely horizontal, creative activity of man, it would be fallacious to regard it as a divine revelation, except in a very large and symbolic sense."[6]

We experience God as divine, not as though he were human with bodily contact points. Hence we do not look for a tap on the shoulder or a whisper in the ear. He contacts us through the effects he produces in our being. What these are we shall discuss shortly. In this sense the experience of God in our present pilgrimage is mediate

<hr>

[5] See, for example, St. Augustine's manner of speaking in *Confessions*, bk. 10, chap. 27. See also St. Teresa of Avila, *Interior Castle*, mansion 6, no. 8.

[6] Piet Fransen, "Divine Revelation: Source of Man's Faith", in Paul Surlis, ed., *Faith: Its Nature and Meaning* (Dublin: Gill and Macmillan, 1972), p. 23.

and indirect. Face-to-face vision is reserved to the home-
land.

Yet we do meet mystics speaking of God granting direct
communications. A St. John of the Cross will call these
"wholly divine and sovereign" communications, "substantial touches of divine union".[7] The word "direct" in
this context seems to be used somewhat differently, that is,
to distinguish these divine touches from the far more indirect knowing of God through objective, transpersonal realities. St. Augustine speaks in this vein also when he
remarks that one can grow to a point where God speaks,
not through finite creation, "but through himself ".[8]

St. Paul undoubtedly enjoyed lofty experiences of God,
and we shall frequently appeal to the apostle for enlightenment on how we may detect the indwelling Spirit working within us and how this inner activity fits with the rest
of the ecclesial enterprise.

What Is Experienced in the Experience of God?

If we can make personal contact with God through the
effects he produces in us, the question immediately arises:
What are these effects? How does God make himself
known? When we examine both Scripture and the mystics, we find that quite a number of distinguishable experiences do occur. I am going to discuss them one by one,
but it should not be therefore concluded that they occur
in neatly discrete packages. It is true that at one time the
experience of God is mainly of one type and at another of
another type, but it is also true that they often inter-
mingle.

[7] *Dark Night of the Soul*, bk. 2, chap. 23, no. 11; p. 385.
[8] *Confessions*, bk. 9, chap. 10; Ryan translation.

1. *An awareness of the divine presence.* In both dispensations, revelation describes God as a God who is present to his people and who makes his presence known. Jesus speaks of the Spirit being present in such manner that we know him because (the causal word should be noted) he is within us (Jn 14:15–17). Jesus promises that he himself will be present all days even to the consummation of the world (Mt 28:20). St. Teresa of Avila refers to the clear consciousness she had of the divine nearness, of knowing that the Lord was at her side in some subtle but unmistakable way, a way that was equally or more certain than that by which we know through the senses of another person's presence.[9]

2. *An awareness senselike and not senselike.* Apparent contradictions are sometimes useful to describe the indescribable. Both Scripture and the mystics use the several senses to describe what a deep encounter with God is like. We are invited to taste and see how good the Lord is (Ps 34:8; 1 Pet 2:3). We learn that Jeremiah felt an inner touch, a fire burning in his bones (Jer 20:9). We are often invited to hear the voice of God speaking. St. Paul speaks of the fragrance of Christ (Eph 5:2), and St. John of the Cross several times refers to "an abundant fragrance" that can appear as a commingling of all the delightful aromas nature can offer.[10] In a splendid passage St. Augustine portrays his experience of God as unlike sense experiences, but then he turns around and says they are like them but far superior. This struggling with paradox is an effort to describe the indescribable.

---

[9] *Interior Castle*, mansion 6, nos. 2 and 8; see also CCC 2709.
[10] *Spiritual Canticle*, st. 17, no. 7; st. 24, no. 6; pp. 480, 504; *Living Flame of Love*, st. 4, no. 4; p. 644.

> Not with doubtful but with sure knowledge do I love you, O Lord. By your Word you have transfixed my heart, and I have loved you. . . . What is it then that I love when I love you? Not bodily beauty, and not temporal glory, not the clear shining light, lovely as it is to our eyes, not the sweet melodies of many-moded songs, not the soft smell of flowers and ointments and perfumes, not manna and honey, not limbs made for the body's embrace, not these do I love when I love my God.
>
> Yet I do love a certain light, a certain voice, a certain odor, a certain food, a certain embrace when I love my God: a light, a voice, an odor, a food, an embrace for the man within me, where his light, which no place can contain, floods into my soul; where he utters words that time does not speed away; where he sends forth an aroma that no wind can scatter; where he provides food that no eating can lessen; where he so clings that satiety does not sunder us. This is what I love when I love my God.[11]

The use of the senses to describe the experience of God is an attempt to insist on the reality of the experience and at the same time to emphasize its richness. One sense does not suffice. Yet the denial that the experience is sensory is an attempt to underline its spiritual character and its superiority.

3. *An infused desire, yearning for God.* Until one is purified sufficiently, he will experience God, not in deep enjoyment, but in a dark desire and yearning. The psalmists write of thirsting, seeking, yearning, longing, panting after God (Ps 42:1–2; 63:1; 119:131). Isaiah does likewise (Is 26:8–9). John of the Cross speaks of experiencing the "void of God".[12] This is not, of course, the emptiness of laziness or laxity. It is a dark contemplative awareness given by God himself and thus an encounter with him.

[11] *Confessions*, bk. 10, chap. 6.

[12] *Spiritual Canticle*, st. 13, no. 1; p. 457.

When we speak of an experience of God, we need to be wary of clear ideas, for God communicates most deeply in dark, general, spiritual manners. There is such a thing as an imaginary detailed vision, but the most lofty communications are wordless and general. For this reason, among others, the mystics together with the biblical writers speak of the ineffability of the experience of the divine (Phil 4:7; 1 Pet 1:8).

4. *Peace and comforting.* The peace of which we speak here is not humanly achieved, nor is it a mere absence of conflict. It is not a satisfaction consequent on getting one's way. These need not be a sign of anything other than merely human factors. We are speaking of a comforting calm that God himself gives (2 Cor 1:3–4), the peace that can become so strong that it surpasses all understanding (Phil 4:7), the peace that is poured in from within (Jn 14:27). This peace shall require close study in a later chapter.

5. *Dark, divine, new knowledge of God.* If one loves Jesus and keeps his commandments, he will receive a new manifestation of the Lord himself (Jn 14:21). The indwelling Father radiates within us a knowledge of his own glory, the glory that shines on the face of Christ (2 Cor 4:6). The mystics uniformly tell us that in their growing prayer they find God in an immense darkness and that the more they find him in this darkness, the better they know that he surpasses all their knowledge. St. John of the Cross looks upon this new "strange kind of knowledge" as unlike anything of everyday life. Many times he wrote of "this loving light . . . this dark light . . . light, simple, pure and general".[13]

6. *Inpoured love from and for God.* Love is central to the encounter of man with God. St. Paul has told us that love

[13] *Dark Night of the Soul,* passim.

is poured out into us by the Holy Spirit who is given (Rom 5:5), and he himself felt driven by this love of Christ (2 Cor 5:14). In his works John of the Cross writes frequently of the living fire of love, of a dark, loving fire, of being passionately in love with God, of walking love-stricken for him. This love is not only the central element in the experience of God, but in its earlier development it is common. A person finds himself loving God with no traceable cause to account for it.

7. *Refreshment.* God's word, says his word, brings new life to the soul, wisdom to the simple, joy to the heart, light for the eye (Ps 19:7–8). The Lord himself remarked that he refreshes the wearied person and satisfies everyone who sorrows (Jer 31:25–26; Mt 11:28–30). St. John of the Cross notes in his own manner that "as a breeze cools and refreshes a man worn out by the heat, so this breeze of love refreshes and renews the soul burning with the fire of love."[14] There are many ways in which one growing in prayer experiences a refreshing inflow from God, but it is to be found even in dark, dry prayer in the form of the peace we have already mentioned.

8. *Being engulfed in God, surrounded by him, immersed in him.* Revelation speaks of God as everywhere, both within and without. The New Testament emphasizes that he is within the Church, within each person as in a temple. And yet both Scripture and the mystics also speak of God as the one in whom we are immersed. God dwells in us and we in him, says 1 John 4:16. Augustine spoke of being encompassed by God on his every side,[15] while Teresa referred to him at her right hand.[16]

---

[14] *Spiritual Canticle*, st. 13, no. 12; p. 461.
[15] *Confessions*, bk. 8, chap. 1.
[16] *Interior Castle*, mansion 6, nos. 2 and 8.

9. *Experience of union and embrace.* Encounter with God includes in its fuller development the experience of being embraced and possessed. St. Paul writes of one who clings to God as being one spirit with him (1 Cor 6:17), and he describes the indwelling presence as including a mutual possession, God of man and man of God (Rom 5:5; 1 Cor 6:19–20). The saints (for example, Thomas Aquinas, Augustine, Angela of Foligno, Teresa, John) routinely mention this aspect of the encounter with the Lord. The last named uses the famous example of the union of starlight with sunlight or of the candle flame with the sunbeam to illustrate the remarkable closeness of this union-possession.

10. *Awareness of the beauty, goodness of God.* He who is touched by God drinks the beauty of God. Psalm 34 and 1 Peter 2:3 invite us to taste and see the very goodness of the Lord. Augustine sings to the inexpressible beauty of the God he loves.[17] St. John of the Cross explains something of the unexplainable: "In this spiritual sense of his presence, He revealed some deep glimpses of His divinity and beauty by which He greatly increased her fervor and desire to see Him. . . . God communicates to her some semi-clear glimpses of His divine beauty."[18] One who encounters God in a genuine experience of him learns firsthand of his beauty as he shares more profoundly in the divine love, joy, knowledge.

11. *Radiant joy in God.* One of the striking differences between biblical literature and almost all secular writing is that the former is saturated with the joy theme, while the latter, though it may speak of pleasure, rarely speaks of joy. The same is true of the difference between the saintly and

---

[17] *Confessions*, bk. 10, chap. 27, and bk. 13, chap. 20.
[18] *Spiritual Canticle*, st. 11, nos. 1, 4; pp. 448–49.

the nonsaintly. The one is full of the tang of life, the other is dull and drab. Psalm 34:5 promises that, if one looks to the Lord, he will be radiant with joy. Isaiah exults for joy in the Lord his God (Is 61:10), and so does the Mother of Jesus (Lk 1:47). St. Paul tells us that the new kingdom consists of joy brought by the Holy Spirit (Rom 14:17), and Peter speaks of a joy in God that is so great that it surpasses descriptive analysis (1 Pet 1:8). Jesus himself declares to his disciples that they would have his own joy, a joy that is complete, that no one can take from them (Jn 15:11; 16:22). The saints so routinely refer to a "burning with delight", experiencing "a marvelous delight" (St. John of the Cross), that I shall merely cite one of them. "Sometimes you admit me", prays Augustine, "in my innermost being into a most extraordinary affection, mounting within me to an indescribable delight. If this is perfected in me, it will be something, I know not what, that will not belong to this life." [19]

12. *The feeling of inner burning.* Some of the traits of the experience of God we have already noted suggest a deep experience indeed. It becomes more apparent why St. Paul insists that only the spiritually mature, the wholly converted can discern the perfect will of God. The rest of us do not have the kind of contact with him that is needed. Our present trait points in this same direction. Jeremiah describes a fire burning in his heart, a fire that he could not bear (Jer 20:9). The disciples on the road to Emmaus likewise refer to a burning within when Jesus explained the Scriptures to them (Lk 24:32). Augustine writes of being set on fire by the psalms,[20] and, noting that he is borne about by love wheresoever he is borne,

---

[19] *Confessions*, bk. 10, chap. 40.
[20] Ibid., bk. 9, chap. 4.

he adds that "by your gift we are enkindled, and we are borne upwards. We glow with inward fire", he writes; "by your fire, by your good fire, we glow with inward fire." [21] John of the Cross speaks simply of "the perfect who burn gently in God". [22]

13. *Power, strength, freedom.* Until one has grown in the life of grace to a considerable extent, he is likely to interpret much of what we have noted thus far in Scripture and the saints as well intentioned but merely pious effusions. He unwittingly measures others by his own mediocrity and so assumes that no one really is radiant with an indescribable delight, that no one really is embraced by God, engulfed in him, immersed in his beauty. So also he is likely to understand the repeated statements about a new strength and power and freedom as enthusiastic effusions. When St. Paul speaks of the power of the Spirit (1 Cor 2:4–5), of the kingdom of God consisting not in mere words but in power (1 Cor 4:20), of wanting to know only Christ and the power of his Resurrection (Phil 3:20), of our possessing an overwhelming power from God (2 Cor 4:7), of our having the very freedom of the Holy Spirit (2 Cor 3:17; Gal 5:13, 18, 22), the mediocre man assumes that this could hardly mean what it says. The saints know better. John of the Cross can write that "the soul obtains [in the strong embrace] not only a very lofty purity and beauty, but also an amazing strength because of the powerful and intimate bond effected between God and her." [23]

---

[21] Ibid., bk. 13, chap. 9.
[22] *Dark Night of the Soul*, bk. 2, chap. 20, no. 4; p. 377.
[23] *Spiritual Canticle*, st. 20–21, no. 1; p. 488.

Implications of the Biblical Account

Perhaps the most striking note of this New Testament picture of how God speaks is the fact that he does not ordinarily speak specifics. It is true that public persons or those closely related to them do occasionally receive particularized directions. This is so of Peter (Acts 10:9–16), Cornelius (Acts 10:3–6), the "Council of Jerusalem" (Acts 15:28), Paul (Acts 9:3–6; Gal 2:2; 2 Cor 12:8–9), Ananias (Acts 9:10–16). In the Christic economy when specific divine messages are given, they must be submitted to human authorities. This has long been the practice of spiritual directors, and it is rooted in revelation itself. Even St. Paul sought the approval of "the leading men" in Jerusalem for the mission he had received directly from the risen Jesus (Gal 2:2, 6, 10). The New Testament gives no comfort to visionaries who deem themselves exempt from any structural approval.

What God usually does speak to the ordinary person is inner transformation. He speaks goodness in a general manner. He speaks his presence . . . spiritual awareness . . . divine-dark knowing of himself . . . yearning for his presence . . . peace and comfort . . . inpoured love . . . union-possession-burning . . . beauty and joy . . . power and freedom. This may come as a surprise to devotees of private revelations, but it does not surprise experienced spiritual directors. Those who listen to God most genuinely are not people who believe they have received many detailed messages, but rather those whose minds have been filled with everything true, noble, good, pure, virtuous and worthy of praise (Phil 4:8).

Types of Communication

God does not speak to us as we speak to one another. He speaks as God, and consequently we should be wary of our preconceived ideas as to how the communication ought to be carried off. Moreover, he does not speak in one way only. Nor should we assume that his speaking is always unmistakable.

The indwelling Lord leads us into all truth (Jn 14:26; 16:13) in diverse ways and degrees. St. John of the Cross discusses these ways and degrees under the caption of what he calls supernatural locutions.[24] It seems to me that this expression, "supernatural locution", is equivalent to what we mean in saying that the Holy Spirit speaks to us. John's "locution" is a type of "apprehension", a knowing. It is a type that is "produced in the souls of spiritual persons without the use of the bodily senses as means".[25] These are not sensory or imaginary visions. They are "produced", that is, received from God. One does not originate the locution. God speaks and enlightens. Man receives.

The saint reduces the many ways in which God speaks to three types. There are, in order of ascending value (and using the saint's terminology), successive, formal and substantial locutions. I will speak of them in my own language as well as John's.

1. *Assisting enlightenment* (successive locutions). This first type of divine speaking always occurs when one is "recollected and attentively absorbed" in some thought process. The enlightenment always concerns the subject on which one is meditating.[26] During this time the person

[24] *Ascent of Mount Carmel.* bk. 2, chaps. 28–31.
[25] Ibid., chap. 28; p. 203.
[26] Ibid., chap. 30, no. 1; p. 208.

is united with the truth and with the Holy Spirit who is in every truth, says John, and yet he is thinking, reasoning in the usual, human manner. The Spirit aids him in forming his concepts and judgments. There is so great a clarity and ease in this activity that it seems another is teaching him, as indeed is the case. In this communion with the indwelling Spirit about a particular matter, the person goes on to "form interiorly and successively other truths".[27] The saint supposes that this enlightenment occurs during prayer, that is, while one is "recollected" and "communing with the divine Spirit". It seems, therefore, that this type of speaking does not usually occur in dialogue sessions but in the midst of prayerful communion.

The recipient of this assisting enlightenment "is unable to believe" that it originates with himself, but he has the awareness that it derives from another. Yet the knowledge received (it cannot be attained by personal industry) is so delicate that the natural intellect by its own activity "easily disturbs and undoes it".[28] This point is important. Even when God does speak in this manner, he does not exclude our human activities with all their limitations, preconceptions, biases, errors. Even when he enlightens, he permits us to be what we as a matter of fact are: fallen—redeemed, yes, but still wounded and deficient.

We may conclude that this assisting enlightenment is not merely human reason proceeding under its own steam and deriving from the Holy Spirit only in the sense that anything true and good derives from him. The divine enlightenment is something over and above the gift of native intelligence, even though in the successive locution it works closely with that intelligence.

[27] Ibid., chap. 29, no. 1; p. 204.
[28] Ibid., chap. 32, no. 4; p. 213.

2. *Independent-ideational speaking* (formal locutions). Whereas the assisting enlightenment occurs only when one is prayerfully meditative, this divine speaking can happen at any time. In the first the locution accompanies human activity, while in the second it is uttered independently of what the recipient is doing: "They are received as though one person were speaking to another."[29] One may receive this locution while he is working, conversing, playing or praying. "Sometimes these words are very explicit and at other times not. They are like ideas spoken to the spirit. . . . At times only one word is spoken, and then again more than one."[30] Although the recipient is clearly aware that this locution comes from another and thus has no reasonable doubt about the otherness of origin, he can only too easily be deceived as to who this other is. It may be God, or it may be the devil,[31] and the discernment is not always easy. Of this I shall speak later.

3. *Dynamic-effective speaking* (substantial locution). It is now well known that the Hebrew idea of "word", *dabar*, was not a mere intellectual representation of reality but a dynamic power. Just as the rain and snow come down from the heavens and produce food, so God's word comes down and achieves its effects (Is 55:10–11). The divine word acts; it does things. It is like fire and a hammer that sunders rocks (Jer 23:29). It is active, alive; it judges, divides and cuts like a two-edged sword (Heb 4:12). Yahweh's word alone caused all creation to be (Gen 1 and 2). Jesus' words are spirit and life (Jn 6:63).

This dynamic-effective speaking (substantial locution) is not merely an assisting enlightenment (the first manner)

---

[29] Ibid., chap. 30, no. 2; p. 208.
[30] Ibid.
[31] Ibid., chap. 30, nos. 3–5; pp. 208–9.

or an ideational speaking (the second manner). It is a powerful producing-in-the-soul of what it says. "For example," notes the saint, "if our Lord should say formally to the soul: 'Be good,' it would immediately be substantially good; or if He should say: 'Love Me,' it would at once have and experience within itself the substance of the love of God; or if He should say to a soul in great fear: 'Do not fear,' it would without delay feel ample fortitude and tranquillity."[32]

These dynamic-effective communications are the most excellent for several reasons. One is that deceit is impossible, since the devil cannot produce this goodness within us. Another is that these locutions impart "incomparable blessings" of life and goodness to the person who receives them. There is consequently nothing to fear or to reject. The recipient need do nothing about them, "because God never grants them for that purpose, but He bestows them in order to accomplish Himself what they express."[33]

Experience of God: A Privilege

When we reflect on the endless gap between infinite and finite, we glimpse at least vaguely how remarkable it is that man should encounter God, should experience something of how he experiences himself, should be able somehow to detect his mind in this encounter. Since discernment does at least in its loftier occurrences imply this experience of God, we ought not to assume that the classical feeling of peace is humanly produced. If perfect discernment demands perfect holiness, it demands what we have been talking about. A deep contact with God be-

[32] Ibid., chap. 31, no. 1; p. 210.
[33] Ibid.

stows a deep perception of his mind. How sublime this contact may be we may illustrate with a few snatches from a single page flowing from the pen of a mystic: "This loving inflow . . . this inflaming and urgent longing of love . . . something immensely rich and delightful . . . this divine fire . . . a living flame . . . this enkindling of love . . . a certain touch of divinity . . . so sublime an experience."[34]

In the sobering remarks I shall be making about the likelihood of illusion among many who feel they are listening to the Spirit, I should not want the impression to be given that genuine experience of God is extraordinary, a thing not to be talked about. Quite the contrary, experiencing the divine is so important that we seek to receive it, yes, but we also wish to deflect counterfeits from it. Since it is the same John of the Cross who will furnish us with strong warnings about deception, we may also allow him to assure us at this point that there do indeed exist remarkable experiences of God indwelling.

Noting that we are called to delight in God in a manner transcending all knowledge and capacity to explain, John issues the invitation: "Come, then, O beautiful soul! Since you know now that your desired Beloved lives hidden within your heart, strive to be really hidden with Him, and you will embrace Him within you and experience Him with loving affection." In this union, says the saint, one experiences a great closeness to God and is instructed in his own wisdom and mysteries. The saint uses all sorts of expressions to articulate some little of what he means: "secret touches of love . . . cauterized by the fire of love . . . it burns up in this flame and fire of love . . . wholly renews it . . . changes its manner of being". He

<hr>

[34] *Dark Night of the Soul*, bk. 2, chap. 12, nos. 4–6; p. 356.

speaks of a "touch of supreme knowledge of the divinity" that cannot be continual or prolonged, for if it were, the person would die. As it is, one "is left dying of love". John feels that so lofty is this experience that only he who has had it can understand it well, and even the recipient cannot explain what he has felt, and so he calls it an "I-don't-know-what".

Authenticity of the Experience of God

We are going to consider in our next chapter illusions and errors as both possible and probable in alleged discerning of the Holy Spirit. We shall likewise devote still other chapters to the revealed signs of who is led by the Spirit and who is not. Nonetheless, we may make several needed observations at this point. And the first is to note how an experience of God may be distinguished from mere emotion. There are several differences. First of all, an emotion originates in some human or finite cause, whereas the experience of God does not. The latter is divinely given and lies beyond the control of the human person (though he can prevent it by neglect or sin). Secondly, the one is heavily of sense, while the other is spiritual, even though the latter can overflow into one's feelings. Thirdly, an emotion never becomes continual, whereas the perception of God does become continual when one has grown fully in him. Fourthly, even the best of emotions do not necessarily produce a new knowledge of God or insight into his economy, while a genuine encounter with him does. Fifthly, emotions are usually neither indelible nor ineffable, while deep experiences of the divine are often both. Sixthly, emotions are not always peaceful, whereas meetings with God carry an inner calm with them. Lastly,

emotions are not necessarily accompanied by moral goodness, while experiences of God do bring a growth in gospel living.

It will be interesting to note that what we are saying
here will be said in biblical thought patterns when further
on we study the signs of authentic discernment. Not
everyone who thinks he is feeling the Spirit *is* feeling the
Spirit.

The question may then be asked whether one can have
a founded certitude that he has met God. Catholic teaching excludes an absolute certainty (unless one has a revelation) of one's being in grace and of final salvation.
Scripture tells us that we are to work out our salvation in
fear and trembling (Phil 2:12) and that we are to hold on
to the grace we have received in reverence and awe (Heb
12:28). The person who considers himself safe should
beware lest he fall (1 Cor 10:12). Yet at the same time
theology does allow for a reasonable assurance that one
possesses the indwelling presence. What I am calling a
reasonable assurance others term a moral certainty or a
practical certitude.

How then do we explain the mystic's certainty that God
dwells within him and that he has really encountered this
God? One answer given is that a deep experience of God
can be equivalent to a revelation and thus can yield an absolute certitude. Another response is that the experience
does not yield absolute certitude but only the well-
founded reasonable assurance, the moral certitude that
excludes reasonable doubts.

God Is Source of Light and Decision

Scripture goes farther than experience. It speaks frequently of God as the very source of light and even the source of our good decisions. We move closer still to the heart of discernment.

God is our lamp, and he enlightens our darkness (Ps 18:28; 27:1; 119:105). He teaches us his statutes (Ps 119:26, 135), for they are light to our eyes (Ps 19:8). The Lord whispers a message into the ears of sinners urging them to change and amend their ways (Job 36:10). He can make his ways known to us, teach us his paths, the paths of integrity (Ps 25:4–5; 27:11; 86:11). He guides the humble to what is right, and he instructs the poor in the divine way (Ps 25:9). God is the very fountain of light, and it is in his light that we see light (Ps 36:9). He sends out his light and truth, and they are to be our guide leading us to his very dwelling (Ps 43:3). In the new dispensation all this is said in trinitarian terms. Jesus is the light of the world (Jn 9:5), and the Holy Spirit whom he sends teaches the disciples all truth (Jn 14:26; 16:13).

The word leads us still more closely to a discerning enlightenment. God gives us a heart to understand, eyes to see and ears to hear (Dt 29:3). He likewise bestows the inner disposition, "the heart", to acknowledge that he is Lord (Jer 24:7). Solomon prays that Yahweh might give him a heart to understand how to discern good and evil in the vast task of leading a large people (1 Kings 3:9). We learn that when one prays, understanding is given him and the spirit of wisdom likewise (Wis 7:7). The Lord gives his servant a tongue with which to speak, and he wakes his servant each morning to listen and hear. This reminds us of Paul's address to the women at Philippi. Luke describes a certain Lydia as hearing the apostle's words, but he notes that the Lord had to touch her heart in order that she might heed the message (Acts 16:14). The same Paul writes to the Philippians that it is God who of his own goodness works within us both the desire and the decision (Phil 2:13). The Spirit so works within us that Paul can say that they are sons of God who are led by the Spirit of God (Rom 8:14).

This being led by the Holy Spirit can grow into a beautiful fullness. St. John of the Cross aids our understanding once again when he describes a state of human operation that has become divine. One of the elements in this transformation is the change from acting through human ideas to acting through divine actuation. The saint explains how after this transformation a person is so thoroughly penetrated by the divine that he remembers something, not because of the ordinary psychological reasons for recall, but because of a direct motion from the Holy Spirit. He notes, too, how in the transformed individual the very first unreasoned movements of his mind and heart are movements under the direction of God and are directed to God.[35] This is indeed a new creation.

A picture of discernment, uncommon in the literature, emerges when one contemplates this transformation of man's powers into a divine manner of operation. The intellect, for example, is no longer moved by humanly achieved light alone but also by a divinely given light. One remembers with a divine memory and loves with a divine love. One lives a new life; he is reborn.

We may say, then, that the enlightened encounter with God is a real meeting of persons and not simply the right

---

[35] *Ascent of Mount Carmel*, bk. 3, chap. 2, nos. 8–12; pp. 216–17.

application of abstract principles somehow taught and learned. One can agree that the responses to God in the discerning process "are bipolar, interpersonal responses to another, not instances of conformity to some predetermined blueprint".[36] They are not mere applications of a universal principle to a concrete problem.

If one chooses to consider this enlightenment by the Holy Spirit as a kind of revelation, we must insist that he sharply distinguish it from public revelation officially guaranteed in the Church by God himself. Further, it is the former that is to be tested by and submitted to the latter, not the other way around. God does intervene in our world. He does enlighten. He does inspire. But private experience can only too easily be illusory, and so we turn our attention to some of the problems a theology of discernment must face.

[36] William Spohn, S.J., "Charismatic Communal Discernment and Ignatian Communities", *The Way*, supplement no. 20 (autumn 1973): 49–50.

4

WHEN DOES GOD SPEAK?

We approach now a problem whose solution is anything but apparent. As a matter of fact, it appears on the surface that the union of two factual premises is impossible. Fact number one: God does speak to certain men and women, and he speaks with unfailing truth. Fact number two: These same men and women are often (not just rarely) mistaken in what they hear or think they hear or in what they conclude from what they hear. We immediately wonder what the sense of fact number one can be, given the existence of fact number two. Why would or should God speak to people who often are mistaken in what they hear or conclude?

One answer to this question is obvious on a moment's reflection. A fruitful source of error in this area is a simple mistaking of the source of the locution. People often think they are listening to the Spirit when he is not speaking at all—or at least he is not saying what they think he is saying. We may not hold God responsible for what he did not say.

Yet a problem remains: Even when God does speak, the recipient may either not hear or distort what he did hear or conclude invalidly from it. Why, then, should

God speak when this may be the likely result? Our response is identical to what we would say about any human speaking to a fellow human: Failure to hear or distortion of the statement or invalid conclusion is always possible. Anyone who has lectured knows this from personal experience. It is remarkable how many people do not hear what you have said (or read what you have written). Yet we do not for that reason cease communicating. God speaks to his people for the same reason we do: many do hear, and hear rightly. A lecturer or writer admittedly takes risks in sharing his thoughts publicly. He knows some will miss the message, while others wittingly or unwittingly will twist it. Yet he also knows that others will hear rightly. God loves us so much that he allows some to distort his word so that he may communicate intimately with those who will not.

Reaction Patterns

It is interesting to observe the widely differing reactions people present to the allegations that the Holy Spirit has spoken to someone or that he commonly enlightens from within. We can speak of a reaction spectrum. At one end of it are those who ridicule the whole idea. They may be theists, but they just do not accept the fact that God says anything particular to anyone. The objectivity of divine revelation is enough for them (though they may forget that the prophets and apostles had subjective experiences of God), and so they look upon charismatic phenomena as a subjective enthusiasm. At the other end of the spectrum are those who readily believe that the Holy Spirit speaks. These people believe that he speaks often and that it is easy to be in touch with him. They tend to be uncritical and are easily persuaded that their thoughts and desires and aspirations derive from a divine source.

Thus our subject is a touchy one. The Church's position lies somewhere between the two extremes of nothing or all. There are valid experiences of God, and they are to be valued. He does enlighten those who are purified sufficiently to perceive his light. But there are also illusory experiences that are nothing more than unfounded persuasions. This raises the problem of subjectivity.

What role ought subjectivity to play in human life? Is life mostly inner perceptions, or is it mainly hard, external facts? Is religion validated by internal experience or by external evidence? Friedrich Schleiermacher located primal religious truth in an undifferentiated experience of absolute dependence, an experience that occurs in one's awareness before consciousness distinguishes clearly between subject and object. When one begins to think and speak about this ultimate dependence, he moves to the level of clear, objective thought, and his expression of it is therefore to some extent at least mixed in with falsification deriving from the everyday objective world. Schleiermacher, therefore, located religious truth, not in doctrinal statements, but in immediate consciousness.[1] This of course lays him open to the charge of subjectivism and relativism. On this basis no one could judge another's doctrinal position. We can easily agree with the comment that

> if the truth is located primarily in present immediate consciousness and only defectively in any type of conceptual expression, then the truth of present consciousness cannot be

[1] These few sentences are a summary of Donal J. Dorr, "Religious Experience and Christian Faith", in Paul Surlis, ed., *Faith: Its Nature and Meaning* (Dublin: Gill and Macmillan, 1972), pp. 73–77.

judged by any religious expressions from the past. This excludes as more ultimate criteria of truth not only dogmas
such as Catholics might invoke but also the appeal to the
scriptural revelation which both Catholics and Protestants
have traditionally made.[2]

To this we shall return later.

Illusions of Subjectivity

While there are people for whom the objective, out-there
fact, rule and norm are everything, there are others for
whom their inner perception, feelings and conscience are
the ultimate criteria of truth. These differences among
people are not to be viewed as unrelated to the problem of
discerning the activities of the indwelling Spirit. If modern biblical and theological advances are teaching us anything, they are making it plain that God takes our
humanness seriously. He even allows his revelation to be
affected by the limitations of our languages, cultures and
individual traits. Since people really do assign differing
roles and emphases to subjectivity and objectivity in their
lives, we see emerging a whole nest of questions about our
ability to discern the Spirit and about the criteria by which
we shall know whether and to what extent we have or have
not detected his finger in our lives.

One does not work long with religiously orientated
people before he meets men and women who are convinced of a personal contact with God and yet who offer
no objective grounds on the basis of which one could give
rational credence to their claims. A theologian may call
this illusory conviction a gnosis, a special knowledge

[2] Ibid., p. 77.

thought to be of God and from him and yet nothing actually more than one's own feelings or insight.

One gets the impression in reading and hearing about widespread practices of "discerning the Spirit" that the whole matter is easy and obvious. But when he looks into the theology of the matter, he finds that our best thinkers take quite another view. They speak of discernment as demanding and difficult. One of the most perceptive of all our writers on the subject of detecting valid and invalid movements of God within the human heart can say:

> Since no one is capable of knowing perfectly the things that pass naturally through his imagination, or of forming an integral and certain judgment about them, how much less is one able to make judgments about supernatural things which transcend our capacity and occur but rarely.[3]

St. John of the Cross is not credulous. He is not persuaded that even on a natural level we grasp completely our inner life, and in this he is more up to date than many of us. It is now common among ethicists to speak of unconscious motivation to explain how we usually do not grasp fully why we do what we do. John's argument is a fortiori: If this is true on the common natural level, it is even more true on the less common supernatural level. He adds that people often think their ideas are from God whereas they are only the product of their own imagination.[4]

A further manifestation of illusory subjectivity is found in the exaggerated individualism we note in much of current ethics. Situation ethics plays down objective norms

---

[3] St. John of the Cross, *Ascent of Mount Carmel*, bk. 3, chap. 8, no. 3; p. 225.

[4] The saint also thought that some diabolically originated ideas are difficult to recognize as such, that is, are difficult to discern. See *Ascent of Mount Carmel*, bk. 2, chap. 29, no. 11; p. 207.

in favor of one's inner love motivation. Almost any physical act can conceivably be good if it occurs in the right circumstances and with the right intention. Karl Rahner and Herbert Vorgrimler are correct in looking upon situation ethics as an "extreme individualism, a short-circuit chosen by a mind that wishes to spare itself the trouble of patient reflection such as is necessary to clarify a complicated situation".[5] It is entirely possible that one may appeal to listening to the Spirit as a substitute for listening to the evidences of study or hearing the Spirit-sent teachers in the Church. We ought not to consider it accidental that young people brought up in this climate conclude to an alarming subjectivity in their ethical opinions. That is good which one feels is good, and hence each is entitled to his own view. We are a long way here from gospel morality.

The illusions of subjectivity find place, too, in prayer life. Many of us fail accurately to assess our growth (or lack of it) in prayer.[6] A few believe themselves to be growing in prayer depth when they are not. Many think themselves stymied in growth when they are advancing nicely. For this reason those attempting to lead a deep prayer life may be well advised to seek guidance from a competent guide (but sadly the evidence suggests that competent guides are few).

Contrary to a fairly common persuasion, excessive subjectivity is a sign of a decadent culture. Even secular writers have noted this in their study of history. "It's an

---

[5] Karl Rahner and Herbert Vorgrimler, *Theological Dictionary* (New York: Herder and Herder, 1965), p. 438.

[6] "Many individuals think they are not praying when, indeed, their prayer is intense. Others place high value on their prayer, while it is little more than nonexistent" (St. John of the Cross, *Ascent of Mount Carmel*, prologue, no. 6; p. 72).

old story", writes one observer, "that in periods of history characterized by quickened erosion of social institutions, of social authorities, there is always a turning within, a pronounced interest in the self, in egoistic states, in reflexive preoccupations. . . . I agree with Goethe that progressive ages are objectivist; subjectivism goes with decadence."[7] Both the individual and society weaken and fragment when they lose a healthy respect for objective evidence and tend instead to seek refuge in experience alone as the criterion of truth. Moral ideals and religious truth, wellsprings of vibrant and creative action, are gone.

Experience in itself begets certainty regarding the experience[8] but not regarding the interpretation of it. This distinction is important for a sound evaluation of supposed listening to God. The illusions of which I am speaking in this chapter are largely due to faulty interpretation of what goes on within one's person.[9] Subjectivity desperately needs objectivity.

Sobriety of Genuine Mystics

The consistent position of the Catholic Church through the centuries has been that one's degree of holiness is securely measured neither by the frequency nor by the variety of inner experiences. The Church has been hard-

[7] Robert Nisbit, *Psychology Today*, December 1973, p. 44.

[8] "An eminent degree of certainty ('evidence') attaches to experience since that which is experienced irresistibly attests its own presence" (Rahner and Vorgrimler, *Theological Dictionary*, p. 162).

[9] "Though our experience of God is doubtless immediate and infallible in its very core, there remains still the very arduous problem of identifying it" (Piet Fransen, "Divine Revelation: Source of Man's Faith", in Surlis, *Faith*, p. 30).

nosed in insisting that sanctity is gauged primarily by deep humility, strong faith, obedient love, even when these virtues are accompanied by no feeling. This is not to belittle valid encounters with God. It is rather to protect them, for they form a vibrant, living dimension of man's whole orientation to the divine.

Through the centuries those who have had the most valid contacts with the Lord counsel the least trust in them. After the biblical prophets and apostles, and together with Augustine, the Gregories, Thomas and Bonaventure, Catherine and Teresa, one would have to place St. John of the Cross at the forefront of those who have had marvelous communications from God coupled with the ability to articulate them. Yet this most reliable and sober of mystics took a dim view of people who are much concerned with receiving extraordinary messages from the Lord. He considered those who desired visions or revelations as guilty of foolishness. He went so far as to recommend that one disbelieve what he receives in a "supernatural way" and rather content himself with believing what the Church teaches and what her reliable ministers say. The saint insisted that all of us be guided through visible channels:

> We must be guided humanly and visibly in all by the law of Christ the man and that of His Church and of His ministers. This is the method of remedying our spiritual ignorances and weaknesses; here we shall find abundant medicine for them all. Any departure from this road is not only curiosity, but extraordinary boldness. One should disbelieve anything coming in a supernatural way, and believe only the teaching of Christ, the man, as I say, and of His ministers, who are men.[10]

---

[10] *Ascent of Mount Carmel*, bk. 2, chap. 22, no. 7; p. 181.

This sobriety will come as a surprise only to those unfamiliar with Scripture. Like John, St. Paul was fully aware of the Holy Spirit's inner enlightenment of the faithful, and yet the apostle often issued visible, human instructions that he expected would be fully followed. We have already noted that Paul received a direct experience of the risen *Kyrios* and yet went up to Jerusalem to confer with "the leading men" and get their approval for his work.

What is our problem then? There are several. What is the use of discernment, if one must clear his decisions with human authorities? Must there really be this clearance? If so, why? Does this not imply a return to the old pyramid approach to ecclesial life where all decisions come from above? If not, why not? Then, too, we may ask what becomes of initiative? We shall address attention to these questions in later chapters. It is important at this point to insist that the sobriety of twenty centuries of the Church's life not be taken lightly.

Our stance, of course, is rather different from the inexperienced enthusiasm of many who believe it is easy to know a genuine inspiration of the Holy Spirit. One writer, for example, considers that the charism of discernment, the capacity to detect the action of the good and alien spirits, is frequently given to a community in its spiritual directors, confessors and leaders in worship. Referring to the impulses of the Spirit in love or peace, impulses that urge one to action, he observes that "many persons notice an enhanced awareness of the guidance of the Spirit in their lives after receiving the baptism of the Holy Spirit."[11] I would agree that many persons feel a

[11] William Spohn, "Charismatic Communal Discernment and Ignatian Communities", *The Way*, supplement no. 20 (autumn 1973): 43–44.

heightened awareness that they ascribe to the Holy Spirit, but that their awareness is actually such may be another matter.

Admixture of Truth and Error

We proceed yet a step farther. Supposing now that a person does validly contact God, we must point out, as we already noted in chapter 2, that even an authentic mystic may unwittingly mingle his own historical or theological errors into a genuine communication from God. This has happened in the past, and there is no reason to suppose that it may not happen today.

We need not look upon all errors as stemming from a diabolical origin or from our own pure selfishness. It is more than remotely possible that any of us may distort a genuine enlightenment from the Holy Spirit. Often enough the divine light is delicate. It does not overpower. It leaves us quite capable even unwittingly of deducing erroneously from it. This is important. Many of us seem to assume that "listening to the Spirit" means hearing neat, specific conclusions that God somehow inserts into the mind. And we further assume that, if we have an idea we think good, it must be he who gave it. Not so. That sort of neat "formulation-insertion" I would call an extraordinary private revelation, not a usual assisting enlightenment. In the latter case, it is we who draw the conclusion, and it may be true or untrue, wise or unwise, loving or unloving.

History bears out the solidity of this analysis. All through the ages there have been men and women who have expressed a profound conviction that their messages, even the most bizarre and untenable messages, have been spoken by God himself. They seem not to suspect that they have themselves contributed anything to their conclusions.[12] In itself the light of the Spirit can never be mistaken. He who is the truth can do nothing but illumine with the truth. However, the light he bestows is often so lofty and delicate that it leaves considerable room for error—unless there be a special divine intervention as is the case with the charism of infallibility given to the Church herself.

Faulty Expressions of Genuine Experience

Still another step is suggested. Supposing now both a valid experience and no admixture of historical or theological error, a further problem may arise: Is the experience correctly expressed? When God does communicate his light to the private person, he does not guarantee that the formulations of that light shall be accurate and free of error. Divine experience in a sincere person by no means excludes the extraneous influences of milieu, background, misinformation, lacunae in knowledge and lack of adequate vocabulary. It has been rightly remarked that "even a genuine revelation (i.e., more than a simple experience of God), occurring in the depths of the soul, may be distorted or misinterpreted by its recipient; religious enthusiasts and sectaries often falsely represent subjective fantasies or sudden manifestations of the subconscious as

[12] "I greatly fear what is happening in these times of ours: If any soul whatever after a bit of meditation has in its recollection one of these locutions [the type the person forms at prayer], it will immediately baptize all as coming from God and with such a supposition say, 'God told me', 'God answered me.' Yet this is not so, but, as we pointed out, these persons themselves are more often the origin of their locution" (*Ascent of Mount Carmel*, bk. 2, chap. 29, no. 4; 204).

private revelations."[13] A discernment of spirits that trusts solely in a subjective contact with God lies open to the aberrations inherent in the human condition.

Thus far we are supposing good will in the person who thinks he is listening to God. When we add the further ingredient of our sinfulness, the very alleged contact with the Holy Spirit frequently becomes doubtful. There must be, therefore, objective criteria by which we may evaluate an encounter with God in prayer or in the active dimensions of life. We all recognize in theory how trivial it is to say that not all "listening to the Spirit" is listening to the Spirit. Only too often it is nothing more than an awareness of our own half-realized desires. This is why we deal later with outer verification.

The obscuring influence of our sinfulness is not always realized. Indeed, it is correct to say that it is usually not realized. Yet its presence is pervasive. Fransen considers that our sinfulness is the chief cause of the misinterpretation of a divine experience. Error and illusion happen, he writes,

> because of the various interfering influences of education, heredity, psychology, language and the culture and doctrine stored in it, but especially because of one's sinfulness. The latter is the only radical menace to the purity of one's interpretation, because it impairs the very roots of the experience itself. Evil is essentially the refusal of God's attraction and love. This refusal makes it more difficult to perceive just what it is we are refusing.[14]

The veteran teacher knows how difficult it is for even adult students accurately to express back to him what they

---

[13] Rahner and Vorgrimler, *Theological Dictionary*, pp. 380–81.
[14] Fransen, "Divine Revelation", p. 33.

have just heard in his lecture. If this liability to faulty expression is frequent in everyday, clear human communications, we should expect its possibility in the dark, divine communications. Our sinfulness as well as our native intellectual limitations readily explain why the expressions of divine experience may be altered by our unrealized pride and preferences.

Diverse Origins of "Inner Lights"

There is yet another aspect to our problem, namely, the origin of the enlightenment. Thus far we have supposed the light to come from God. Our theology of discernment of spirits speaks in the plural: spirits. While most people are willing to grant that their own biases and preferences may suggest ideas to their minds, a goodly number may merely smile at the suggestion that the devil may be their origin. Even though this is not the place to adduce the ample biblical and magisterial evidences for diabolical reality and activity, it may be useful to point out that we do not pick and choose among the data of divine revelation. Sound exegesis by all means. But nonetheless one accepts the whole Christ message, or one shows that his criterion of acceptance is his own judgment rather than the divine word. The *Catechism of the Catholic Church* states that "the existence of the spiritual, non-corporeal beings that Sacred Scripture usually calls 'angels' is a truth of faith. The witness of Scripture is as clear as the unanimity of Tradition" (CCC 328). After a review of biblical evidence, the Scripture scholar Leopold Sabourin concludes that "whoever reads the New Testament without preconceptions or myth phobia should easily agree" that there is clear evidence of the existence of a personal hostile power and that this is an essential element in New Testament teaching. Sabourin also refers to Lyonnet's judgment regarding St. Paul's assertion on the devil: "To conclude from these passages that Satan is for the Apostle a pure personification of the forces of evil would be to contradict as a whole the biblical and Pauline doctrine." [15] Our best theologians write in the same vein. "The existence of angels", writes one of them, "cannot be disputed in view of the conciliar declarations (D 428, 1783). Consequently it will be firmly maintained that the existence of angels and demons is affirmed in Scripture and is not merely assumed as a hypothesis which we could drop today." [16]

"Scripture witnesses to the disastrous influence of the one Jesus calls 'a murderer from the beginning', who would even try to divert Jesus from the mission received from his Father. 'The reason the Son of God appeared was to destroy the works of the devil.' In its consequences the gravest of these works was the mendacious seduction that led man to disobey God" (CCC 394). As the *Catechism* points out, the power of Satan is not infinite, "although Satan may act in the world out of hatred for God and his kingdom in Christ Jesus, and although his action may cause grave injuries—of a spiritual nature and, indirectly, even of a physical nature—to each man and to society" (CCC 395). It is indisputable that we are subject to temptations and that discernment is essential.

If inner enlightenment may originate in other than divine sources, questions arise. Can we know in a trustworthy manner the origin of our inner lights and aspirations?

[15] Leopold Sabourin, "The Miracles of Jesus (II). Jesus and the Evil Powers", *Biblical Theology Bulletin*, June 1974, p. 153.

[16] Karl Rahner, "Angels", *Sacramentum Mundi* (New York: Herder and Herder, 1969–1970), 1:32.

Does the Holy Spirit make himself known? How do we detect him? What are the signs of his activity as distinguished from diabolical machinations?

Depreciation of Intellect and Objectivity

One further problem remains. It is the exaggeration of religious experience out of all due proportion. As I write this paragraph I am reminded of a lecture I gave four or five days ago. During the ensuing discussion period, I pointed out to a questioner that she was rejecting something clearly taught by the Magisterium (and not disputed among Catholic theologians). Her response to my previous reasoned presentation and to this external authority was: My experience is otherwise; I have nothing else to go by. Her position is, of course, illuminism. Evidence does not penetrate the illuminist mind. Subjective "experience" rules out objective fact.

Once one maintains that we can have a conscious contact with God and thus discern his guidance, one must face up to the question of how we can distinguish a valid contact from an imaginary one. That the question is not idle may be seen from the number of aberrations that have occurred in the last four centuries. To me it is significant that the aberrations are typically accompanied by a depreciation of intellect and reason. For Luther, man is passive in his justification even though he experiences a conviction of it. Faith is no longer an intellectual assent to doctrines but a trust in salvation. For Calvin, salvation happens through the touch of the Holy Spirit, and one's experience of affective satisfaction in these touches assures him of their authenticity. Jansenism depreciated theoretical reason and extolled affectivity so that "the soul was represented as capable of an immediate feeling of the rapport between itself and God." [17] Schleiermacher regarded speculative reason as superstition and religious experience as "a purely emotive state resulting in an immediate impression of the divine". [18] The modernist movement at the turn of the last century belittled dogmas as norms for truth and held instead that this latter (truth) emerged from the subjectivity of the human person.

Discernment is incarnational. It has an inner element and an outer element, not just one or the other. Inspiration of the Holy Spirit does not substitute for faith or hierarchy. Problems arise in history when authorities stifle the Spirit or when people who think themselves led by the Spirit cast aside the hierarchy. Subjectivity demands the direction of objectivity. This we discuss later under the rubric of verification.

[17] W. J. Hill, "Experience, Religious", NCE 5:752.
[18] Ibid.

PART TWO

POSSIBILITY OF DISCERNMENT

5

CRITICAL DISCRIMINATION

Because our God is a hidden God, and because we are burdened with countless illusory desires and imaginings, it is by no means easy to ascertain whence come our inclinations, projects and decisions. And yet the quality of those inclinations, projects and decisions depends considerably on their origins. For this reason discernment is largely a matter of detecting sources, "the spirits".

What Are the Spirits?

The biblical concept of spirit, *ruah* (Hebrew) or *pneuma* (Greek), is richly variegated, as it is also in modern languages (see CCC 691). *Ruah* referred at times to the movement of air, either of wind (Is 30:33, where the wind is the burning breath of Yahweh; or Ezek 19:12, where he is in the gentle breeze) or of the breathing of a man. In this latter sense, at creation the Lord breathes into the first man the breath of life (Gen 2:7), for it is the breathing of Shaddai that gives man his life (Job 33:4) and forms his spirit within him (Zech 12:1; Wis 15:11). At death this spirit returns to the Lord, who gave it (Qo 12:7). It is he who takes it away (Tob 3:6; Bar 2:17).

When God sends forth his spirit, things are created and he renews the face of the earth, puts things together (Judith 16:17; Ps 104:29–30; Ezek 37:5–14). When the human person gives up his spirit in death, he gives up his life and consciousness and power.

This mysterious *ruah* in man can faint, be troubled, bitter, crushed or angry (Ps 77:3; Gen 41:8; Gen 26:35; 1 Kings 21:5). Furthermore, the human person finds other powers or forces entering his being: the spirit of discord (Jg 9:23), impurity (Zech 13:2), jealousy (Nb 5:14), prostitution (Hos 4:12), giddiness (Is 19:14), lies (1 Kings 22:19–23), lethargy (Is 29:10), justice, judgment, courage (Is 28:6). While good spirits are of Yahweh, evil spirits are also from him (1 Sam 16:14)—the Israelite ascribes everything to God as the ultimate cause of all that is.

The *ruah* of Yahweh in the Old Testament is a power that gives men strength (Micah 3:8), accompanies their prophetic mission (Is 61:1; Ezek 2:2), enters into and raises up the prophet (Ezek 3:12, 14, 24; 8:3, 11:1). The spirit of Yahweh speaks through the prophet (2 Sam 23:2; Zech 7:12) and takes hold of a leader (1 Chron 12:18). It can even be shared among leaders (Nb 11:17). The spirit of the Lord is to be poured out in the messianic age on all mankind (Joel 3:2), and a new heart and a new spirit are to be created in them (Ezek 36:26–27). The spirit of the Lord in the Old Testament can take men and transform them so that they do deeds far surpassing their native ability. Samson, Gideon and Saul are thus transformed for their special roles in freeing their people. Othniel is possessed by the spirit of the Lord, becomes a judge in Israel and goes out to fight for his people (Jg 3:9–10). The spirit of Yahweh seizes Saul, and his "fury was stirred to a fierce flame" (1 Sam 11:6). In a special manner God gives his *ruah* to leaders.

The New Testament *pneuma* continues many of the Old Testament usages of spirit. It is a source of human life that leaves at death (Mt 27:50). Paul contrasts spirit with flesh, the former being a principle of goodness and life, the latter of sin, corruption and death. The apostle also uses the term as equivalent to soul and the source of mental activities[1] (1 Cor 7:34; 16:18; 2 Cor 2:13; 7:1, 5). There is of course the evil spirit, Satan. The New Testament testifies to Jesus' struggle against Satan's kingdom (Mk 1:12–13, 23–28; Lk 8:26–39; 10:17–20; Jn 13:2, 27; 14:30; 16:11). The disciples, too, must beware of the devil who seeks those whom he may devour (1 Pet 5:8–9). He tempts us and attempts to bring us to sin (1 Th 3:5; 1 Cor 7:5). He tries to outwit us (2 Cor 2:11), entrap us (1 Tim 3:7), ensnare us by his tactics (Eph 6:11). He makes war on the children of the woman (Rev 12:17). Yet the Lamb and his people will finally overcome him.

Most importantly in the New Testament, the *pneuma* is the Holy Spirit himself sent by the Father and the Son. Of this Divine Person we say much elsewhere in these pages, and so we need only to mention him in this place.

"Dokimazete ta pneumata"—*"Test the Spirits"* *(1 Jn 4:1)*

It would be simplistic to think that the biblical concept of discernment may be adequately derived from an analysis of the one or two word groups that are translated by the English "discernment". Yet at the same time we should take a careful look at the Greek expressions that are used

[1] Cf. John L. McKenzie, *Dictionary of the Bible* (New York: Macmillan Pub. Co., and London: Collier Macmillan, 1965), p. 844.

in the New Testament to speak of testing, approving, learning, dividing.[2]

The Greek word *diakrisis* refers to distinguishing, dividing and judging, and it is used for discerning the spirits, for evaluating whence comes a particular communication. Paul speaks in 1 Corinthians 12:10 of a gift of recognizing spirits, and he lists it among sundry other charisms given to the faithful: preaching, faith, healing, working miracles, tongues and such like. The community is admonished in 1 Corinthians 14:29 to test the origin of the alleged communications from the prophets.

The *dokimazein* word group occurs frequently both in the Gospels and in the Epistles. The verb *dokimazein* occurs twenty-two times in the New Testament, with seventeen of these uses being in St. Paul.[3] In classical Greek it most often means to test, prove, discern money or men or wine—to judge something good or worthy. In the Septuagint it translates several Hebrew words:[4] *bahar*, to choose, select; *hagar*, to scrutinize deeply or examine; *iaqar*, precious, magnificent; *saraf*, to purify (metal from its impurities), to test and thus select the best. Through Hebrew influence it signifies examination, testing, purifying, getting to know the deep reality of a person or thing, detecting what is better.[5]

[2] See Gerard Therrien, C.Ss.R., *Le Discernement dans les écrits pauliniens* (Paris: J. Gabalda, 1973); Friedrich Buechsel, *"Diakrino, Diakrisis"*, in Gerhard Kittel, *Theological Dictionary of the New Testament*, ed. Geoffrey W. Bromiley, vol. 3 (Grand Rapids, Mich.: Eerdmans, 1966), pp. 946–50; Walter Grundmann, *"Dokimos"*, Kittel, *Theological Dictionary of the New Testament*, vol. 2 (Grand Rapids, Mich.: Eerdmans, 1964), pp. 255–60.

[3] Lk 12:56 twice; 14:19; 1 Cor 3:13; 11:28; 16:3; 2 Cor 8:8, 22; 13:5; Rom 1:28; 2:18; 12:2; 14:22; Phil 1:10; Eph 5:10; Gal 6:4; 1 Th 2:4 twice; 5:21; 1 Tim 3:10; 1 Pet 1:7; 1 Jn 4:1.

[4] See Therrien, *Discernement*, pp. 17–18.

[5] Ibid., p. 19.

A related verb, *apodokimazein*, occurs nine times in the New Testament, none of them being in St. Paul.[6] It refers to a rejection following a testing. The noun *dokime* and the adjective *dokimos* occur seven times each.[7] The root, *doke*, means sentinel, one who watches and judges who may be admitted into the camp. The word therefore means tested, authentic, worthy of being trusted.[8] The adjective *adokimos* occurs eight times in the New Testament[9] and is used of worthless money or bad men. The noun or adjective *dokinzos* refers to an index, that which is authentic, and it occurs only twice.[10] The noun *dokimasia* occurs only in Hebrews 3:9. It is a legal term and refers to an examination of aptitude of public officials and priests.

The New Testament affords little comfort to illuminists. While it is convinced of the Holy Spirit's manifold operations in the Church, it demands that alleged phenomena be put to the test. Authenticity is not readily assumed.

The Biblical "Two Ways"

Despite the numerous problems entailed in reckoning with religious experience, the New Testament is optimistic in holding that we can contact God and that we can know when that contact is authentic and when it is imaginary. It may be helpful to summarize the rich biblical terminology for distinguishing the two ways, for this is fundamentally a discerning of spirits.

[6] Mt 21:42; Mk 8:31; 12:10; Lk 9:22; 17:25; 20:17; 1 Pet 2:4, 7; Heb 12:17.
[7] *Dokime*: Rom 5:4 twice; 2 Cor 2:9; 8:2; 9:13; Phil 2:22; *dokimos*: Rom 14:18; 16:10; 1 Cor 11:19; 2 Cor 10:18; 13:7; 2 Tim 2:15; James 1:12.
[8] Grundmann, *"Dokimos"*, p. 258; Therrien, *Discernement*, p. 10.
[9] Rom 1:28; 1 Cor 9:27; 2 Cor 13:5, 6, 7; 2 Tim 3:8; Titus 1:16; Heb 6:8.
[10] James 1:3; 1 Pet 1:7.

There are four expressions, couplet expressions, for designating the two ways in both the Old and the New Testaments. The most common is the distinction between the *righteous* (the good, blameless, faithful) and the *wicked* (Ps 1:1, 6; 101:2, 6; 119:30; Prov 2:20–22; 4:14, 18–19; 8:20; Sir 21:10; 1 Sam 12:23; 1 Kings 8:36; Is 59:8; Lk 1:79; James 3:17–18). Then there are those who walk in the *light* and those who stumble in the *darkness* (Prov 4:18–19; Lk 1:79; Jn 3:19–21; 11:9–10; 12:35–36; 1 Jn 1:6–7; Eph 5:8; 2 Cor 6:14–7:1). In the last text, while Paul does not forbid every contact with the pagan world, he does rule out any minimizing of the vast differences between the disciple of Jesus and the pagan of Corinth.[11] A third expression to distinguish the two ways is the contrast between *truth* and *error* (as also between the true prophet and the false one) (Prov 12:28; Tob 1:3; 2 Th 2:12; 1 Jn 4:1; 2 Pet 2:1–2). Regarding 1 John 4:1–6, Wilhelm Thusing remarks that "according to the author of 1 John and indeed the whole of the New Testament, those who proclaimed a religious message were in the service of a spirit. Either the 'spirit of truth' or the 'spirit of error' was speaking from them."[12] The author of 2 Peter notes that just as there were false prophets in the past history of God's people, so there will be false teachers in the present. These men disrupt the community, disown the Master, destroy themselves and bring the Way of Truth into disrepute (2 Pet 2:1–2).[13] The final con-

---

[11] "In this pagan city many Christians desire more accommodations with the pagan world. . . . The attempt to efface the distinction between Christian and pagan in daily life is disastrous" (Tomas O'Curraoin, *A New Catholic Commentary on Holy Scripture* (London: Nelson, 1969), p. 1169.

[12] Wilhelm Thusing. *The Three Epistles of St. John*, NTSR 23 (London: Sheed and Ward, 1971), p. 72.

[13] Regarding this text, Alois Stoger remarks, "God permits false prophets in his church to test his people on their undivided love of him and their

trast frequent in and common to both Testaments is the *life–death* contrast: one road leads to full living, the other to self-destruction (Prov 2:19; 5:6; 6:23; 12:28; 15:24; 2 Cor 2:16). It is frightening to realize that the holy word of God not only brings life to those receptive to it but that it also occasions greater evil in those who resist it. "For the believers, who are on the road to salvation, the perfume of the preaching vivifies, and intensifies that life; for those who are on the road to perdition, who prefer darkness and death (Jn 3:20–21), the preaching drives deeper into evil and death."[14] The word of truth divides the two ways. The proclamation of the Church occasions the great cleavage in the world between the two camps.

We find two contrasts infrequently mentioned, namely, that between the *wheat* and the *straw* or *weeds* (Jer 23:28; Mt 13:24–30) and between the *pure* and the *guilty* (Prov 21:8).

The New Testament adds a rich variety of new expressions that distinguish the person on the right path from the one on the wrong. The first clings to *God's will*, the second follows *human passions* (1 Pet 4:2). The one goes by the *hard road* and the *narrow gate* leading to life, while the other enters upon the *wide and easy road* leading to perdition (Mt 7:13–14). *Men of the Spirit* are interested in spiritual things, promote love and unity, while *men of the flesh* are interested in worldly matters, cause factions and disharmony and impurity (Rom 8:5–9; Jude 19; Gal 5:16–22). The latter simply cannot understand the things of God (1 Cor 2:14).[15]

---

ability to distinguish between truth and error" (*The Second Epistle of Peter*, NTSR 22 [London: Burns and Oates, 1969], p. 156).

[14] Tomas O'Curraoin, in *New Catholic Commentary*, p. 1166.

[15] On this text John O'Rourke comments, "The 'natural' *psychikos* man is he who does not possess the Spirit, he who relies on natural resources only" (*New Catholic Commentary*, p. 1146).

There are contrasts between the *saved* and the *lost* (2 Cor 2:15), that which is *from above* and that which is *from below* (Jn 8:23), *divine wisdom* and *human learning* (1 Cor 2:6–7), the *humble* and the *proud* (Mt 11:25), the *holy* and the *sinful* (1 Jn 3:1–10), *vision* and *blindness* (Jn 9:39),[16] God and the *Evil One* (1 Jn 5:19; Eph 6:11–12), *virtue* and *crime* (2 Cor 6:14),[17] the *presence of love* and the *absence of love* (1 Cor 13:1– 3), the *new creation* and the *old creation* (2 Cor 5:17; Mt 13:52), those concerned with *invisible* realities and those concerned only with *visible* things (2 Cor 4:18). Regarding a text similar to this last, 1 John 2:17, Bruce Vawter comments that "whoever belongs to this world and its desires has committed himself to an order that 'is passing away.' Opposed to it is 'he who does the will of God,' who thereby possesses the eternal life because of which he 'abides forever.'"[18]

We may summarize the fundamental New Testament discrimination of the two ways by the repeated contrast between *God* and the *world*, the latter taken in its pejorative sense common in both the Johannine and Pauline writings but found elsewhere as well. The authentic disciple is not of this world just as Jesus is not of it (Jn 8:23; 17:16), and so the world hates him as it hated Jesus (Jn 17:14). We are admonished not to love either "this passing world or anything in it, for the love of the Father cannot be in any-

---

[16] Jesus discriminates between "'those who do not see', the humble who, like the blind man, confess their ignorance; 'those who see', the 'know-alls' whose smug satisfaction destroys their spiritual vision" (Ralph Russell, *New Catholic Commentary*, pp. 1056–57).

[17] Karl Schelkle notes that in 2 Corinthians 6:14–16 St. Paul with a stylistic *tour de force* shows with no less than five phrases that a conformity between believers and unbelievers is impossible (*The Second Epistle to the Corinthians*, NTSR 14 [London: Burns and Oates, 1969], p. 101).

[18] Bruce Vawter, in JBC 62:15.

one who loves the world" (1 Jn 2:15). They who have the Holy Spirit do not have the spirit of the world (note the explicit sign of discernment), and they embrace the foolishness of God rather than the wisdom of the world (1 Cor 2:12; 3:18–19). Holy men and women do not model their lives on the behavior of the world, but they change to holiness in Christ and are thus enabled to detect the perfect will of God (Rom 12:2). This is so true that they consider themselves strangers and pilgrims on the face of the earth (1 Pet 2:11). "The Christian is by vocation an alien and exile on this earth."[19] James makes the contrast between the two ways starkly clear: "To make the world your friend is to make God your enemy" (James 4:4).[20]

We already have, therefore, in rough fashion a biblical doctrine of discernment. How do we tell one who is led by God from one led by himself, by the world, by the Evil One? The answer, clear but not yet fully explicit, may be shown by a simple summary of the biblical formulations of the two ways:

The one way is the way of the	The other way is the way of the
—righteous	—wicked
—light	—darkness
—truth	—error
—genuine prophet	—false prophet
—life	—death

[19] W. J. Dalton, in *New Catholic Commentary*, p. 1249.
[20] This sharp separation is rooted in the Old Testament. Commenting on Deuteronomy 6:4–5, W. L. Moran remarks, "In committing a man without reservation to the 'one Yahweh', Dt separates a man from all that is of this world as radically as Yahweh is distinct from any other god" (*New Catholic Commentary*, p. 265).

—wheat	—straw (weeds)
—pure	—guilty
—God's will	—human passions
—narrow gate	—wide gate
—hard road	—easy road
—Spirit	—flesh
—saved	—lost
—from above	—from below
—divine wisdom	—human learning
—humble	—proud
—holy	—sinful
—vision	—blindness
—God	—Evil One
—virtue	—crime
—presence of love	—absence of love
—new creation	—old creation
—invisible things	—visible things
—God	—world

The person led by the Spirit of God is thus one who teaches and lives a sacrificial way of life; he is pure and humble and loving; he argues from a divine wisdom from above and is concerned with God's will; the morality he teaches is a hard road, but it leads to a new creation; he argues from the invisible things of God. The person led by the spirit of the world teaches and lives an easy, soft way of life; he is impure, proud, unloving; he argues from human learning and favors human passions rather than God's will; the morality he teaches is an easy road, but there is nothing new about it. Most people accept it. He reasons from visible realities rather than from the invisible.

There are then two ways clearly demarcated in Scripture, and they can be distinguished. Yet a further task remains: the spirits that prompt the ways, the origins, must themselves be noted and tested.

The Spirits Must Be Distinguished

The paths we men and women tread have an origin and an orientation. The orientation depends on the origin. Whether we choose to orientate our lives and our individual actions to the first elements in each of the above couplets or to the second (and each set forms a consistent pattern) depends on whether we are being spurred to action by God, on the one hand, or by our native selfishness (or the devil), on the other. The New Testament writers are sensitive to this problem of testing origins, the spirits, of what we do and what we omit.

This critical discrimination receives most attention in the Pauline and Johannine traditions. In the earliest of the New Testament writings we find that the faithful are not to quench or suppress the Spirit, but at the same time they are to test everything and distinguish good from evil: "*Panta dokimazete*"—"test all things" (1 Th 5:21). St. Paul teaches that there are two spirits operating in the world: one the spirit of death and slavery, the other the spirit of life and adoptive sonship. Those who live according to the deeds of the body will die, whereas those who are led by the Holy Spirit and put to death the deeds of the body will live freely as sons of the Father (Rom 8:13–16). It is possible, says the apostle, to distinguish the spirit of the world from the Spirit of God. A person led by the former just cannot grasp the truth taught by the latter (1 Cor 2:12–15). Whether one is acting under the influence of the Holy Spirit can be determined by his doctrinal attitude toward Jesus. Just as one cannot confess the lordship of Jesus except under the influence of God's Spirit, so also one who curses the Lord cannot be speaking by the influence of this Spirit (1 Cor 12:3).

While the pilgrim people of the new dispensation should generally be able to discern the Spirit (if they are holy and sanctified sufficiently), there are some who are gifted with what seems to be a special charism of discriminating between spirits. St. Paul numbers among the charisms given in the Church (the context speaks of miracles, prophecy, tongues) that of "the ability to distinguish between spirits" (1 Cor 12:10). Commentators are not of one mind as to the precise meaning of this ability, whether it is an ordinary or an extraordinary gift. The *Catechism of the Catholic Church* reminds us that whether they are extraordinary or humble, "charisms are graces of the Holy Spirit which directly or indirectly benefit the Church, ordered as they are to her building up, to the good of men, and to the needs of the world. Charisms are to be accepted with gratitude by the person who receives them and by all members of the Church as well. . . . [D]iscernment of charisms is always necessary. No charism is exempt from being referred and submitted to the Church's Shepherds" (CCC 799–801).

Our capacity to discriminate between the two ways is implied in the gospel conviction that good and evil can be known through their effects. A prophet, for example, can control his spirit and so should contribute to communal calm, for the true God is a God not of confusion but of peace (1 Cor 14:32–33). Those who are children of light can be distinguished from children of darkness, for the results of light are visible for all to see. Thus we can truly discover what God wants of us (Eph 5:8–10).

Like the Pauline literature, the Johannine urges the distinction between good and evil men by the doctrine they hold and teach, for "no lie can come from the truth" (1 Jn 2:21–24). Thus one who clings to the tradition of what has been proclaimed in the Church will have the Holy Spirit and will share life in the Son. The good and evil spirits can be distinguished also by whether one keeps the commandments or not, especially the new commandment of loving the brothers as Jesus loves them (1 Jn 3:10, 24; cf. Jn 13:35). James, too, teaches that the two ways can be distinguished by deeds. The one way is characterized by gentleness, humility, peace, purity, mercy, certainty and sincerity, whereas the other produces jealousy, ambition, pride, disorder and insincerity (James 3:13–18).

The most explicit statement in Scripture that the true Spirit can be distinguished from the false occurs at the beginning of a brief treatise on discernment. "Beloved, do not believe every spirit," cautions the Johannine writer, "but test the spirits to see whether they are of God; for many false prophets have gone out into the world" (1 Jn 4:1). There then follows a summation of Johannine thought on how we may detect the false and the true: the former profess erroneous doctrine and refuse to obey their leaders in the faith, while the latter possess true doctrine and listen to those who articulate the community's teaching (1 Jn 4:2–6). This idea is expressed twice in the one letter. In this last text we read that the world shows that it is not of God in its refusal to heed his spokesmen (1 Jn 4:6). In another we learn that men refuse the proclamation of the Church because they have previously refused God himself (1 Jn 3:1).

In a text full of mystery we find that somehow one can know how he stands with the Father through the very indwelling presence of the Holy Spirit (1 Jn 4:13; cf. 1 Jn 5:20). Likewise emanating from the Johannine school, the message to the angel of the church of Ephesus includes the observation that you "have tested those who call themselves apostles but are not, and found them to be false" (Rev 2:2 RSV).

Yet a further point must be made. Inner separation from the Spirit living in the Church is sometimes shown by outer separation from the believing community. Antichrists, rivals of the Lord, show that they never did belong to him when they leave his Church. Speaking of these opponents of the Lord, 1 John notes that "they went out from us, but they were not of us; for if they had been of us, they would have continued with us; but they went out, that it might be plain that they all are not of us" (1 Jn 2:19 RSV). The New American Bible identifies these antichrists as "all the false teachers who afflict the church in the final hour". One who is of the Spirit of God remains within the unity of the *ekklesia* that the Son himself has founded. Departing from the visible unity is a sign of a previous departure from the invisible oneness established by the indwelling Spirit.[21]

But there is still another separation-sign, namely, that imposed by the leaders of the *ekklesia* upon one who stubbornly refuses to be healed of a serious fault. Discriminating between the true and the false brother reaches the point where, upon refusal to be corrected in a serious matter, the erring disciple is officially excluded from the community. If one refuses to be corrected privately and then semiprivately and finally before the community itself, he

---

[21] Bruce Vawter remarks on 1 John 2:19: "The false teachers who have separated themselves from the Church never truly shared in the Church's life of God. The author speaks of this as a self-evident fact to which Christian experience must testify. Apostasy is its own proof that the apostate never possessed the spirit of Christianity" (JBC 62:16).

is to be separated from the faithful (Mt 18:15–18). This exclusion is seen as an excessive discipline only if one fails to appreciate the gospel insistence on unity in belief and practice (1 Cor 1:10f.; Phil 2:1–2; Acts 2:42; 4:32). Trilling, commenting on this passage, says that "this directive with regard to a sinning brother sounds harsh. Its severity can only be properly understood when the serious nature of the pastoral charge is grasped."[22]

Problems Not Insuperable

We have suggested that the experience of God is a privilege. It is. It is a remarkable privilege. We have, however, said that this privilege may be beset with all sorts of illusions of subjectivity. This also is only too true. History, past and present, is our witness. Discrimination, healthy discrimination, is thus indispensable.

We have noted that the New Testament in diverse ways indicates that the authentic can be separated from the inauthentic, and both can be known for what they are. This is the core of discernment in a nutshell.

Practical Suggestions

Supposing, then, that they are sons of God who are led by the Spirit of God (Rom 8:14), and yet that all things are to be tested (1 Th 5:19–22), we may ask what this biblical position requires in everyday life. How does one tread the path of the golden mean between two extremes?

  1. *Hard-nosed evidence.* While we should value the divine interventions in our world, we should not suppose

[22] Wolfgang Trilling, *The Gospel according to St. Matthew*, NTSR 1–2 (London: Burns and Oates, 1969), 2:95.

them unless the biblical conditions are fulfilled. We do not presume, for example, that a proud, vain person is listening to the Spirit. Jesus has made it clear that the Father does not reveal his mysteries to the conceited but only to little ones. A competent spiritual director looks for gospel holiness before he accepts that his client is "listening to the Spirit". This is why for centuries knowledgeable directors have discounted alleged divine phenomena in proud or disobedient people. They who reject the outer word cannot be hearing the inner word. God does not contradict himself.

2. *No finite idea expresses God adequately, and thus we ought not to cling to it.* One of the most valuable contributions offered by St. John of the Cross to this question of listening to God's voice can be missed even in a careful study of his work. It is that the most important element in most divine communications is not the clear idea, the detailed course of action to be followed. It is the love-penetrated touch of the divine in dark faith, a touch that itself communicates humility, love, prayer, strength, peace, joy. The most valuable gift God can share with anyone is himself. And he is no thing, no idea, no pattern of action. The Love who is God is poured out into our hearts by the Holy Spirit who is given to us (Rom 5:5). Once we understand this, we have gone a long way in understanding John's severity in making so little of locutions and visions. The saint recommends that the recipient of divine communications pay little attention to them, because if he gets attached to them, he feeds on them rather than on God.[23] One likewise begins to consider himself especially

---

[23] The total renunciation demanded by Jesus is applicable here: "Unless a man renounce all he possesses he cannot be my disciple" (Lk 14:33). Even an idea about God is not God.

favored by God and to look down on others who, in his opinion, do not enjoy this same enlightenment by the Spirit. The attachment can become a stubborn refusal to listen to anyone who may disagree because "I am listening to God." Clinging to a finite communication, this person fails to "soar to the heights of dark faith".[24] And in pilgrimage it is only in faith that we journey to the fatherland (Heb 11:13–16).

3. *Little attention is to be given to inner communications.* I suspect that many people are surprised by, if not shocked at, the attitude St. John of the Cross takes toward inner enlightenments. He repeatedly advises the recipient to pay little attention, even no attention, to them. The saint is so strong on this point that, unless one is well acquainted with his whole life and teaching, he might conclude that John scarcely believed that God does communicate with men. Yet he deeply believed in this communication and in his own person enjoyed the very loftiest types of it.

Because his teaching is surprising to many of us, it may be well to offer a summation of it. We may first note two examples typical of the saint's statements of rejection, and then we will consider several reasons for them. Speaking of imaginative visions or "other supernatural communications" received by the senses and independent of one's free will, John asserts: "I affirm that at whatever time or season (in the state of perfection or one less perfect) an individual must not desire to give them admittance, even though they come from God."[25] Later on in the same work as he discusses successive locutions, the saint again says, "We should pay no heed to them, but be . . . content

---

[24] St. John of the Cross, *Ascent of Mount Carmel*, bk. 2, chap. 18, no. 2; p. 160.

[25] Ibid., chap. 17, no. 7; p. 158.

with knowing the mysteries and truths in the simplicity and verity with which the Church proposes them." [26]

This advice admittedly runs counter to what most of us would expect. We would think that if God speaks, we should pay attention, close attention. We would consider a rejection of the communication an insult to the speaker of it. Why is John of this mind?

The first reason is the likelihood of illusion, deception. St. John of the Cross would surely agree that when God speaks, we should listen carefully. This is precisely why he clings so tenaciously to Scripture and to the teaching Church. Public revelation is sure and free from illusion and so is the teaching of the divinely commissioned Church, pillar of truth (1 Tim 3:15). Private revelation is often not sure, that is, what is commonly thought to be revealed by God is not revealed at all. St. Paul was of this same mind. He told the Galatians in no uncertain terms that even if an angel from heaven were to teach them something contrary to what they learned from human lips, they were to reject it (Gal 1:6–9). In other words, Paul was saying that such private "revelation" was not revelation at all. When one pays much attention to "communications" he leaves the sure path of faith for the unsure path of "what I heard, what I received, what I see". History tells a long and sad tale of the illusions that abound in this second path.

Secondly, people who are much concerned with God speaking within tend to neglect clear duties without. "On judgment day," says our Carmelite guide, "God will punish the faults and sins of many with whom He communed familiarly here below and to whom He imparted much

---

[26] Ibid., chap. 29, no. 12; p. 207.

light and power. For they neglected their obligations and trusted in their converse with Him."[27] John then illustrates his idea with the words of Jesus, "When that day comes, many will plead with me, 'Lord, Lord, have we not prophesied in your name? Have we not exorcised demons by its power? Did we not do many miracles in your name as well?' Then I will declare to them solemnly, 'I never knew you. Out of my sight, you evildoers!'" (Mt 7:22–23). Doing the Father's will (Mt 7:21) is more important than receiving special favors from him. St. Paul repeats this truth when he tells the Corinthians that their most marvelous charisms (including the gifts of healing, miracles, tongues) are of no value without love (1 Cor 13:1–3). The Carmelite explains how spiritual directors should guide people in faith, not in supposed special communications.

A third reason is core. The deepest value in a divine communication does not lie in clear concepts or blueprints for future action. It lies in a deeper drinking of the divine, a drinking that is general, dark, nonconceptual, love-immersed. If a person pays much attention to the clear words or ideas he has "heard" at prayer, he is absorbed in finite particulars rather than with the God who is infinitely beyond the best of our concepts. In pilgrimage we journey to the fatherland best not in clear ideas, but in dark faith.

Paying little attention to communications is wise, fourthly, because a subtle vanity easily seeps into people preoccupied with "listening to the Spirit" in a self-conscious way. Like the Pharisee in the parable (Lk 18:9–14), they may begin to consider themselves unlike the rest

---

[27] Ibid., chap. 22, no. 15; p. 185.

of men. Needless to say, this attitude is not conducive to growth in love.

Fifthly, giving attention to inner communications carries with it the need to discern their origin. Do they come from God really or from the devil or from one's own unrealized desires? While the work of discernment is advisable for important matters, one can hardly seek out a spiritual guide and/or engage in long discernment processes for routine daily affairs. If one is an avid "listener to messages", the alternatives are a preoccupation with analysis or an unfounded assumption that "it all comes from the Lord." Even a saint does not assume the latter.

Finally, the recipient of an authentic communication from God does not need to pay attention to it in order to derive its benefits. This many people do not realize. God produces the good effects of his communication without the recipient being able to prevent it. "A person", says John of the Cross, "cannot hinder the goods God desires to impart, nor in fact does he do so, except by some imperfection or possessiveness." [28] By renouncing all divine communications (and John includes visions, locutions, fragrances, pleasures, words), "a person takes from these apprehensions only what God wants him to take, that is, the spirit of devotion, since God gives them for no other principal reason." [29] The same is true of the lesser assisting enlightenment. [30]

Paying little attention to inner enlightenments is for all these reasons a sensible reaction that combines a vivid

---

[28] Ibid., chap. 17, no. 7; p. 158.

[29] Ibid., no. 9; p. 159.

[30] "The profit produced by a successive locution will not be received from focusing one's attention on it. Through such behavior a person instead would be driving away the locution" (ibid., chap. 29, no. 7; p. 205).

faith in the indwelling Spirit with a sober refusal to succumb to a credulous illuminism. These reasons also explain the remaining bits of practical advice.

4. *Use of reason as a source of light.* God expects us to use ordinary means to achieve ordinary ends. If I break a leg, he expects me to get it set by a doctor. I may pray for divine healing but not instead of refusing ordinary medical help. We should surely pray for divine enlightenment but not instead of refusing study and consultation. Where human reason is sufficient to solve problems, God is not likely to intervene in a supernatural manner.[31]

5. *A divine message needs human approval.* This advice is shocking. It seems a reversal of the truth: a human message needs divine approval. A distinction is in order. When the divine message is public, it needs no approval other than that required by Christ himself. That is, it needs the acceptance of no merely human court. St. Paul explicitly declared that it made not the slightest difference to him whether any human tribunal found him worthy or not (1 Cor 4:3). Yet the same apostle submits his divinely received commission from the risen Lord to the authorities in Jerusalem (Gal 2:2, 6, 10). All the more when a divine message is a private revelation must it be approved by due authority (see CCC 801).

The New Testament consistently requires supposedly divine communications to be submitted to the approval of the Lord's representatives. This we already find in the earliest New Testament document. The gifts of the Spirit are not to be suppressed, but they are to be tested (1 Th 5:19–22). Those who want to hear Jesus must be prepared to hear his representatives; otherwise they are rejecting him

---

[31] Ibid., chap. 22, no. 13; p. 184.

(Lk 10:16; Jn 13:20). The heretics at the close of the first century are known to be false prophets because they refuse to listen to the leaders of the *ekklesia* (1 Jn 4:1, 6).

In the work of spiritual direction, I consistently find that persons who give every sign of genuine prayer development and authentic holiness instinctively follow this practice. The Holy Spirit gives them the inner inclination, even a felt need, to submit the apparently divine communication to a priest in whom they can confide.[32] This inclination may be taken as a sign of a genuine communication from God, whereas its absence suggests otherwise.[33]

This advice is, of course, consistent with all else we have studied here. Christ did not establish an angelism, an invisible Church. He takes our bodyliness seriously. He operates now both immediately through his Holy Spirit working invisibly and mediately through human representatives working visibly. So great is the likelihood of illusion and misinterpretation in the subjective realm that an objective evaluation is indispensable. What should be done when a competent guide is not available we consider next.

6. *Competent spiritual direction*. A qualified and experienced guide when faced with alleged divine communica-

---

[32] "God is so content that the rule and direction of man be through other men, and that a person be governed by natural reason, that He definitely does not want us to bestow entire credence upon His supernatural communications, or be confirmed in their strength and security until they pass through this human channel of the mouth of man. As often as He reveals something to a person, He confers upon his soul a kind of inclination to manifest this to the appropriate person" (ibid., chap. 22, no. 9; p. 182).

[33] The saint connects this trait with humility: "This is the trait of a humble person: he does not dare deal with God independently, nor can he be completely satisfied without human counsel and direction" (ibid., chap. 22, no. 11; p. 183).

tions sees them in their context. He considers the recipient's way of life, whether it is characterized by love, joy, humility, detachment, and obedience. The Father and the Son do not reveal themselves to the unloving, the proud, the disobedient (Jn 14:21; Lk 10:21). St. Paul told the Galatians that what the Spirit brings to his own is not self-indulgence or temper or factions or impurity but rather love, joy, peace, patience, gentleness, self-control (Gal 5:19–22). In our own day it remains true that a deep prayer life, a genuine communion with God indwelling, is invariably accompanied by these New Testament criteria.

People still complain, however, as did St. Teresa of Avila four centuries ago, of the lack of knowledgeable spiritual guides. What should one do if he cannot find a competent director? It is my opinion that in the area of advancing prayer, as also in this matter of alleged communications, no direction is preferable to probably incompetent direction. A great deal of damage can be done by well-intentioned but inept advice. If one thinks he may have some enlightenment from God but can find no one competent with whom to share it, it is best just to turn one's attention from the communication and speak of it to no one.[34]

7. *Growth in faith.* A pilgrim people travels not by vision but by faith (Heb 11:13–16; 1 Cor 13:12). When God deals with private persons, he usually communicates with them in the general knowledge of dark faith. Even if he should offer a specific message, he wants it confirmed by the appropriate human authority.

The proximate means by which we are united to God is nothing finite and created. It is the adherence to God himself revealed in his word. The stronger this clinging to

[34] Ibid., chap. 30, no. 5; p. 209.

him, the more readily he communicates with the one clinging. For St. Paul, only the converted, the holy can detect the mind of God. The more we are transformed by faith and love, the more God can pour out additional light and love into our hearts and minds. In this way we are transformed from one glory to another by the indwelling Spirit (2 Cor 3:18).

6

THE CONDITIONS FOR DISCERNMENT

Discernment is demanding. Not everyone who wishes to detect the motions of the Holy Spirit does detect them. Diligent dialoguing, even when interspersed with earnest prayer, is no necessarily sure path to the divine mind. Techniques and processes may be useful, but, like recipes, without ingredients they are useless.

God's criteria for enlightenment are radically different from ours. We relate understanding and insight with research and libraries and grants and universities and lectures and doctorates and microfilm and computer retrieval systems. Our view of the matter is often correct about specifics, the factual. It is almost entirely wrong about basics, the ultimate, the fundamental evaluation of the human situation and what to do about it.

Few would disagree that the knowledge explosion has had negligible effect on the world's supply of wisdom. Many have given up as naïve their earlier trust in scientific solutions to fundamental problems. Those who still cling desperately to science as salvation meet rude shocks each day in the morning newspaper.

Nor is philosophy much more helpful. Although genuine philosophical thinking does penetrate to the ultimate level of human reason, it does not and it cannot solve the radical puzzle of human existence. Once again we have as proof not only our own contemporary experience but centuries of earnest endeavor, sometimes brilliant endeavor. There is one answer and one answer alone. Without God we are hopeless.

But we are not without God. He has intervened in our world by proclaiming a word into the human family in various and diverse manners in times past. In our last ages he has spoken his last Word, after which there remains nothing more to be said in public revelation. Yet this Lord continues to speak privately, also in various and diverse manners. He does enlighten and inspire and guide from the deep recesses of the person who says a complete Yes to the enlightenment, the inspiration, the guidance. God whispers into the listening ear. He gives to the receptive. He gifts the ready.

But who is ready? That is our present problem.

We have reflected on the problematics of discernment. We have noted that it is not at all obvious that all "listening to the Spirit" is listening to the Spirit. We have considered that subjectivity is open to all sorts of illusion even in well-intentioned people. We have just said that discernment is demanding.

This is why receptivity and readiness are crucial. Only one who is rightly disposed can detect the gentle motions of God working in his heart and mind. We turn, therefore, to the revealed word to inquire of it who the receptive may be. We ask of revelation: Who is the ready?

Revelation responds that not everyone is prepared to listen to the indwelling Spirit. One gets the feeling from the divine message that the one who is most inclined to think he is listening to the Lord God is the least likely to be tuned into him, whereas the one who considers himself of small account, who is prepared to obey a human superior, is the very one who really is listening to God. Once again, his ways are not ours.

And so we ask of the divine word: Who is ready to listen to the whisper of the Lord?

The Humble Hear

Anyone who hopes to detect the mind of God, to hear him, to learn his ways and to probe his will must expect to be surprised, even to be contradicted. Most of us would expect that the way to the mind of infinite Truth is diligent study, a searching out of wisdom, ancient and new. This is a way, but it is not *the* way. The first condition for detecting the divine mind is just what we would not expect: smallness, unpretentiousness, apparent weakness.

The Simple See

Humility is transparent; pride is opaque. There is a realism in the peasant that often escapes the prince. Scripture has it that the simple understand God's word as it unfolds; its lightsomeness penetrates into their persons (Ps 119:130). Those who proclaim the word see this in their work. One and the same homily or lecture occasions enthusiastic acceptance in some, hostility or indifference in others.

Humility precedes honor (Prov 18:12). Only the little ones gain entrance into the kingdom of Christ (Mt 18:3–4; 19:14)—and, I may add, into his mind. Anyone who wishes to rank first with him must be the last and the servant of all (Mk 9:35). Thus the humble possess wisdom (Prov 11:2), and the proud do not. The former are men and women of faith, and they therefore walk in a security free from the illusions of petty desires. In a letter to Doña Juana de Pedraza, St. John of the Cross tells her that she was never better off, because she was never so small, so humble in her own sight. Because she is in darkness illumined by faith, she is secure from error. She is in darkness a propos of her own reasoning, from which so many mistakes emerge, and because she is now walking "along the road of the law of God and of the Church" she is preserved from the deceptions caused by illusory desires.[1]

The simple see likewise because they are ready to turn to God for a solution to their problem. We read that a humble, lowly people seek refuge in Yahweh. They do no wrong and speak no lies (Zeph 3:12–13). They do not meddle in what lies beyond human understanding, beyond their duty (Sir 3:23).

Pride is opaque. If humility precedes honor, pride comes before destruction; haughtiness precedes a fall (Prov 16:18). There is little hope for the man who is wise in his own eyes (Prov 26:12). He is so sure of his thoughts and his ways that he cannot conceive that there is any other thought or any other way. And he is more than a little confident that his thought and his ways are God's inspiration. It is difficult for him to learn the lesson that the divine is above the human as the heavens are above the earth. This is one reason among others why he so easily considers that he is listening to the Spirit. The divine transcendence has not quite penetrated.

The proud often do not think of themselves as proud. They have more favorable and pleasant characterizations to describe their views and their decisions. The opacity of

---

[1] Letter no. 19; p. 699.

pride is usually couched in euphemistic terms, terms favorable to the speaker. One who refuses to obey a superior surely will not describe his behavior as selfish or self-opinionated. No, he is simply being mature. He refuses to cooperate with power structures. He will not buy into a system that fails to respect persons. He is exercising coresponsibility (on his terms), and he is taking the future into his own hands. Rejection of hierarchical directives is rewritten as being responsible to the people of God. Refusal to obey liturgical norms is said to be a pastoral sensitivity to people's real needs. There is an aura of holiness about it all.

God Gifts the Humble with a New Light

Humility is a condition for discernment not only because the simple see, that is, because there is a readiness in their very persons, but also because God chooses to bestow on them what he denies to the arrogant. If I may presume an attempt to explain why God does what he does here, I would say that he favors the little because they are honest. They are real. God loves realism.

It is a general principle in the biblical revelation that God offers the humble a special access to his gifts (Prov 3:34). He listens to their wants, brings strength to their hearts, grants them a hearing (Ps 10:17). The greater one is, the more he should behave humbly, for then he finds favor with the Lord.[2] The *Catechism of the Catholic Church* reminds us that "*humility* is the foundation of prayer" (CCC 2559).

---

[2] See Joachim Jeremias, *Rediscovering the Parables* (New York: Scribner's, 1966), pp. 114–15.

The proud, on the other hand, are in a bad way. Because pride is "the reservoir of sin, a source which runs over with vice" (Sir 10:13 NAB), God destroys the haughty utterly. He overturns the thrones of the arrogant, plucks up their roots, breaks down their stems to ground level, effaces their very memory from the face of the earth. The imagery is devastating. The humble he seats in the place of the mighty and plants them in their stead (Sir 10:14–17; Lk 1:52). The Lord raises the latter on high (James 4:10).

Why are the arrogant wicked? Why does the Lord God resist them, close his bounteous hand from them? Their sin begins with stubbornness, with a prior withdrawing of their heart from the Lord (Sir 10:12). Because they are evil and thus refuse to serve God, the day is coming when they shall be so burned up like stubble that they will have neither root nor branch (Malachi 3:18–19). We may lay it down as a principle that God resists the proud and showers his gifts on the lowly (James 4:6; 1 Pet 5:5). St. John of the Cross explains that "communications which are truly from God have this trait: they simultaneously exalt and humble the soul."[3] One who is genuinely of God is gradually enriched with the divine abundance, and at the same time he grows in humility. He knows God better and is therefore exalted; he knows himself better and is consequently humbled.

Yet Scripture says more. It not only makes the general statement that the Lord showers goodness on the little ones, but it likewise teaches that he sheds on them the specific goodness of his own light. This makes explicit that humility is a condition for getting to the divine mind.

---

[3] *Dark Night of the Soul*, bk. 2, chap. 1, no. 2; p. 371.

The humble man knows where the source of light is. He trusts completely in Yahweh and places little confidence in his own insights (Prov 3:5). He is aware that only the fool trusts his own mind (Prov 28:26). God rewards this realism. He guides the humble in all that is right; he instructs the poor in the divine way (Ps 25:9). The prophet who really has the word of the Lord imitates John the Baptist, who decreases that his Master may increase. Isaiah, too, "almost completely submerged himself in giving voice to the word communicated by the Spirit".[4] The man of the Spirit is small in his own eyes, and he is glad to be small that the Lord may be great in his life.

Jesus repeats the same message. The Father enlightens the merest children, the babes, while he hides his mysteries from those wise in their own conceits (Lk 10:21; Mt 11:25–26). Wolfgang Trilling can comment on this policy that "it seems almost as though God had a preference, even a sort of weakness, for those who do not count for anything in the world."[5] There is a basic reason for this weakness. The proud are full of their self-importance and their light. They have no room for God's way and wisdom. He leaves them to their full emptiness.

Humility is both a preparation for the Spirit and a result of the Spirit. Not only does the Paraclete choose to enlighten those who are not inflated with their own importance, but it is his very light that enables one to be humble. When God begins to pour his dark contemplation into our mind and heart, we begin to perceive more and more clearly both his purity and our sinfulness, his

[4] Bruce Vawter, *The Conscience of Israel* (New York: Sheed and Ward, 1961), p. 165.
[5] Wolfgang Trilling, *The Gospel according to St. Matthew*, NTSR 1–2 (London: Burns and Oates, 1969), 1:211.

limitlessness and our finitude. This is why humility is an excellent index of our depth in God, of our prayer and of our insight.

From this simplicity also emerges the joy of the Holy Spirit, the joy of which St. Luke so often writes. Regarding the attainment of the simplicity of the least in prayer, Pope Paul VI remarked that "then you will experience the joy of one who exults in the Holy Spirit, the joy proper to those who have been introduced into the secrets of the King."[6] He is the fountain of joy. There is no other.

The Conformisms of Pride

Pride is a tyranny. The world teems with examples. One of the most striking is the slavery of the man who is concerned about the opinions of others, the man who wants to make a good impression, the man who so lives in the minds of others that he cannot live in his own mind. Styles in clothing offer an obvious example of tyrannical conformism. Many men and women, perhaps most, choose styles, not for their inherent value for warmth, convenience or modesty, but for the purpose of "looking beautiful". Only God knows how many suits, coats, dresses (and much else) are bought, not because the present suit, coat or dress is worn out, but simply because it has been seen fairly often or because Parisian designers have decreed that lapels shall be wider or skirts shorter. Which is a frightful tyranny when one reflects for a moment on the millions in the world who have no wardrobe at all and who today are starving and dying at the rate of ten thousand per day.

[6] *Evangelica testificatio*, Apostolic Exhortation on the Renewal of Religious Life, no. 54.

Most of us are such meek conformists that we see nothing amiss in changing with the spring and fall styles and letting our naked brothers and sisters in Asia and Africa and Latin America (and in parts of our own Western world as well) go without one decent change of clothing. We are such meek conformists that we lower and raise hemlines simply because a decree has gone out of Paris or London or New York. We buy new clothing because "they say" this or that is the new chic style. What "they" say is more important to us than what the Gospel says: "If anyone has two tunics he must share with the man who has none, and the one with something to eat must do the same" (Lk 3:11). We are such meek conformists that few of us dare to run counter to the assumptions of the department-store show windows. And clothing is only one example of the tyranny of vanity. In differing ways the same phenomenon is found in our decisions about cars and rugs and drapes and appliances and grooming and travel and dining and drinking . . . and who could not add to the list?

Yes, the proud live in the mind of others. There is no room for the mind of God, a mind that is dead set against the mainstream of secular society. The proud cannot detect the motions of the Spirit because their minds are impregnated with another value system, and value systems exclude one another. Jesus could assert that human approval meant nothing to him, that his listeners could not believe because they sought approval from one another, not from God (Jn 5:41, 44). Concern for human approval blocks divine approval.

The Humble Listen

The haughty may speak much of openness and listening to others, but they do mighty little of it. Humility is a condition for discernment because God speaks not only through his inner enlightenment but also through men and women, especially through those he himself has commissioned to teach and correct in his Church. The humble person is open to being corrected, whereas the arrogant is clearly closed to it. Proud people are supremely confident in their own opinions and insights. No one can admonish them successfully: not a peer, not a local superior, not even the pope himself. *They* know—and that is the end of the matter. Filled as they are with their own views, the arrogant lack the capacity to see another view. Their typical response to an admonition, even an admonition well fortified with evidence, is either an analysis of the person who spoke it or a dismissal by labeling or a rejection by caricature. Or all three.

The humble listen to their brothers and sisters because they assume they have something to learn. They are open to correction, and they become wiser through it. They come closer to the mind of God himself. Scripture says a great deal about all this—and in terms stronger than I am using. We shall deal with this biblical theme further on.

A Sign of Authenticity

Though we shall not directly consider humility in our later section on signs of the Holy Spirit, it could easily be placed there. Through the long centuries of the Christian dispensation, spiritual directors have considered humility as an important sign of authenticity. When St. John of the

Cross was asked his opinion of a nun who reportedly had extraordinary experiences, his analysis of her written account was negative because indications of humility were lacking. She had, he said, little fear of being mistaken. She was overly confident of her opinion. Where this healthy fear is absent, remarked the saint, the Spirit of God is never present. She seemed to desire to persuade others of the goodness of her experiences; she gave little evidence of humility, and her style lacked simplicity—it was exaggerated and affected. The saint was consequently little impressed with her experiences.[7]

In the concrete order humility shows itself as a sign of the Spirit's operation in several ways. It appears in the desire to be corrected. It shows itself in the avoidance of the self-focusing of illuminism. The humble person can be reached by objective evidence because he does not consider himself a privileged channel from the Holy Spirit to the human race. It is a chilling experience to meet face to face with a person so supremely sure of his inner light and his interpretation of the Bible that he rejects not only what you say but also what exegetes and theologians and saints say. He rejects these interpreters, unaware that he is setting himself up as the interpreter par excellence.

This humility sign is seen in obedience to one's legitimate superior and to one's spiritual director. This person has no problem about submitting his will to that of another. The humble individual is willing to be sent. He is not a self-originating oracle. If he is the recipient of a genuine divine communication, even if his leaders think otherwise, he still obeys.

---

[7] *Complete Works*, p. 683.

Listening and Correcting

We men are amusing in more ways than one. At one moment in our history a particular idea is unpopular, frowned upon. Ten years later someone gives it a new attractive name, and the newly dressed concept is accepted. It may even become the new "in" proclamation. The idea of docility is a case in point. The word means, of course, a capacity to learn, to be taught by another. Yet in recent years the idea came upon hard days, for it spoke to many of a passivity, a weakness, a refusal to think for oneself. But then on the scene came a new label: openness, listening. Now openness and listening to others mean nothing if they do not mean exactly what docility means: willingness to be informed, instructed, changed by what another says.

But here we have a problem. Not everything that is called openness *is* openness. Often the word is a euphemism for "accept what I say; it is right because I say it." What is not expressed but implied is "I need not accept what you say, because you are wrong." It is much like the popular "we must be free and responsible for our own actions." This was highly esteemed and practiced until those who proclaimed it got into positions of authority. At that point those who disagreed with them were "divisive", and freedom now meant embracing the new orthodoxy.

God speaks in many ways: in the rustle of a breeze, the rising of the sun, the smile of a friend. But he speaks mostly in his revealed word spoken in ancient days through the prophets and in these last days in his very own Son, the radiant image of his glory. Our concern here is to discover how this Lord speaks to us in our brothers and sisters who are filled with the wisdom of Christ (Col 3:16). These, the wisdom-filled, are vehicles to us of the mind of the Lord. We are ready to discover the mysteries of the Father when we are ready to be admonished by those who are close to him, who love him and thus know him (1 Jn 4:7–8).

Authenticity and Admonition

Scripture has a great deal to say about what we call listening to our brother and sister. Biblical writers were less ambiguous than we, and so they used plain terms: being instructed, admonished, corrected. They did not speak in vague generalities that contained little substance. And they surely did not believe in a "listening" that did not include a willingness to be affected and changed by what is heard. For biblical men, one listened to another when that other's word did something to him. This use of language is quite different from much of our own. For us, one "listens" when he is sophisticatedly attentive, superficially sympathetic, polite. Not so for the ancient Hebrew.

The authentic man not only accepts instruction from another, he clings to it, for this instruction is his life (Prov 4:13). He not only welcomes reproof, but he also takes it seriously; he is affected and changed by it (Prov 15:5). A son is to listen to the instructions given by his father and his mother (Prov 1:8; 4:1, 10, 13; 6:20–23). A wise son welcomes correction, but the senseless one rejects it (Prov 13:1). These are plain words.

A man in trouble laments that he did not listen to his teachers, and thus he finds himself in a sad state, utter ruin (Prov 5:12–14). A candid admission of a blunder is refreshing and not often heard in human affairs. It is the saint alone who is large-minded enough to think and speak in this way. This is part of his authenticity.

The person who is swift to hear and slow to respond (Sir 5:13) is a stranger to an all-knowing illuminism. He believes that others, too, have some truth, and he is willing to be instructed by them. He is ready for the mind of God.

Correction Not Optional

The biblical concept of fraternal correction is rich, multifaceted. We may consider it from four points of view: the simple fact, the why, the how, the results.

First the fact: healing the erring brother is a necessity, for it can prevent the occurrence of evil (Sir 19:12–13). St. Paul wants the Colossians to teach and admonish one another (Col 3:16), and he trusts that the Romans can give advice to one another (Rom 15:14). If someone is found in sin, the "spiritual" among the Galatians should gently set him right (Gal 6:1). Jude wishes the brothers to correct the confused in their community (Jude 22). Jesus himself had already said that if a brother offends, one is to go to him and admonish him in order to win him back to health (Mt 18:15f.).

Why correction? Mutual healing is part of a whole picture of warm fraternal concern: cheering the fainthearted, supporting the weak, never returning evil for evil, always seeking the other's good, admonishing the unruly (1 Th 5:14–15). Only the rugged individualist refuses brotherly correction. We admonish, therefore, not to hurt or to get revenge. Our aim is healing one we love, preventing the brother from further hurting himself or the community. But there are other purposes, too. A presbyter who sins is to be reprimanded publicly as a deterrent to others doing likewise (1 Tim 5:19–20). The omission of a necessary correction may result in future harm: one who winks at faults causes trouble (Prov 10:10).

How to correct? It is in this "how" that we make many of our mistakes. How do we avoid them? First of all, we are to correct gently and with patience (2 Tim 2:25). Although the pastoral Letters and the Johannine literature are uncompromising in their concern for the truth and even advise separation from the unrepentant who cling to their errors (for example, 2 Tim 3:5), yet there is also need for gentleness in trying to win the erring sister or brother.[8] The Thessalonians, says Paul, are to correct "as a brother" anyone who disobeys the apostle's directions (2 Th 3:15). A second important "how" is privacy. When one errs, I am to go to him alone as the first step, and only if he refuses to be healed do I bring the matter to the attention of others in the community (Mt 18:15–18). Finally, we are to be informed: we admonish "in all wisdom" (Col 3:16). A disciple of the Lord is not getting revenge on an enemy or merely releasing pent-up emotions when he corrects. Because he is healing a wounded brother, he is knowledgeable. He knows what he is about. He brings the wisdom of God to the sister or brother.

The results? Fraternal admonition "in all wisdom" obviously brings the wisdom of the Father. It is a source leading one to the mind of the Lord. Thus the neglect of taking counsel leads to failure, whereas consultation leads to success (Prov 15:22). Correction of children brings wisdom to them and eventual comfort and delight to their parents (Prov 29:15–17). Candid correction brings peace to the community (Prov 10:10).

[8] See Joseph Reuss, *The Second Epistle to Timothy*, NTSR 19 (London: Burns and Oates, 1969), p. 145.

Wisdom Welcomes Correction

We proceed a step further. We are to welcome instruction, yes. But this is not enough. We are to welcome correction as well, being told that we are wrong. This is living the virtue of docility.

As the word indicates, docility is the capacity to learn, a willingness to be taught. One is docile when he recognizes his own lack of information and expertise, on the one hand, and the superior knowledge and skills of his teacher, on the other. In this context a synonym more acceptable to modern ears is receptivity.

There are two types of receptivity: one toward the indwelling Spirit and the other toward human teachers. Like other moral virtues, docility lies in a mean between two extremes. One extreme is the more or less arrogant refusal to accept the thoughts of another. The other is an exaggerated credulity that has lost a sense of proper discrimination and healthy criticism.

The ancient Semite could be refreshingly blunt. He surely was blunt when he came to speak of wise and foolish men. He terms the person who hates reproof stupid. Period. The one who loves reproof loves knowledge (Prov 1:7; 12:1). Correction is a source of learning; it brings wisdom (Prov 15:31–32; 19:20). The reason we reject correction is plain pride: "He who corrects an arrogant man earns insult. . . . Reprove not an arrogant man, lest he hate you; reprove a wise man, and he will love you. . . . He becomes wiser still" (Prov 9:7–9 JB). The arrogant man is doomed; his work is fruitless and worthless (Wis 3:11). This rejection of correction brings woe to the rebellious and alienation from God: "She hears no voice, accepts no correction; in the Lord she has not trusted, to her God she has not drawn near" (Zeph 3:1–2 NAB). It likewise brings poverty and shame (Prov 13:18) and allows one to go astray (Prov 10:17).

The rejection of correction can take the form of active hostility. After Jesus had exposed the hypocrisy of the Pharisees and lawyers, one might have thought that they would engage in some self-examination and repent. But no, they were not interested in the truth. After Jesus had left the gathering, says Luke, they "began to manifest fierce hostility to him" and contrive traps to catch him in his speech (Lk 11:53–54). Stoger comments on this episode, "The root of the lawyers' crime lay in the fact that they had set up their own wisdom, not God's word, as the center of everything."[9] Only the humble accept being informed, whereas the foolish man is convinced that he is right: "The way of the fool seems right in his own eyes. . . . The fool is reckless and sure of himself" (Prov 12:15; 14:16 NAB). He therefore spurns the correction of another (Prov 15:5). He despises the wisdom of a genuinely good, intelligent man (Prov 23:9). As Paul would have it, he just cannot understand (1 Cor 2:14).

It is typical of a saint that he will accept correction even from an unworthy person. Our greatest writers and thinkers are eager to be evaluated by others and to bend to the judgment of the magisterial office. One recalls the astonishing accomplishments of Francis Xavier, who read letters from his superior on his knees. We note how modern feminists pale next to Catherine of Siena, who operated on an international scale and with a complete obedience. We remember how Bridget of Sweden "did not hesitate to remind kings, political rulers, prelates and people of their

---

[9] Alois Stoger, *The Gospel according to St. Luke*, NTSR 5–6 (London: Burns and Oates, 1969), 1:23.

duties. She worked indefatigably for peace in Sweden, France, Italy and England." We read of her, "It would be difficult to name a place in Europe which did not feel the influence of her activity for temporal peace and religious reform." [10] And this woman was a mystic.

[10] John Cardinal Wright, "Reflections on Saint Birgitta", *L'Osservatore Romano*, October 25, 1973, p. 5.

PART THREE

SIGNS OF THE HOLY SPIRIT

7

MORAL BEHAVIOR

We are prepared now to take up the practical problem of identifying authenticity in the real world of human persons, opinions and movements. How do we know when one is being led by nothing less exciting than the Spirit of the living God rather than by nothing more dull than one's own hidden aspirations? Given the fact of unconscious motivation, how do I know myself that I am actually being enlightened by God indwelling rather than by my own wounded intellect and will? In a pluralistic world, how does one sift the wheat from the chaff?

Humanly speaking the task is impossible. The long history of ideas makes it clear that the most brilliant minds cannot by themselves attain untarnished truth. In our own day anyone who reads widely and with some humility (that is, anyone who does not out of sheer arrogance embrace an artificial certitude) can easily despair of discovering truth in the welter of opinions expressed both in the mass media and in serious books and journals. Left to ourselves, we are not only unable to attain authenticity, we cannot even know it in any complete manner.

Yet Scripture does offer a complete set of criteria for detecting truth, especially religious and moral truth. We shall deal with the wealth of biblical thought by considering, first, its general principle and, then, its concrete applications.

General Principle

Authenticity begets goodness: From their fruits you shall know them. Scripture plays on this theme in many ways as it distinguishes the genuine from the ungenuine. Foolishness and evil gush forth from the heart of the wicked (Prov 12:23; 15:28). The holy man speaks little, and when he does converse, his words reflect his holiness; they are controlled, measured, sensible, without sin (Prov 10:19; 11:12; 12:16; 17:27; Mt 12:36). Inner goodness shows itself in outer words.

The New Testament is explicit. Just as a good tree produces good fruit, so does the good man produce goodness from his inner spirit. "From the abundance of the heart the mouth speaks" (Lk 6:43–45). By looking at their fruits, the faithful can discern the false from the true prophets (Mt 7:15f.; 12:34–35). Wolfgang Trilling, commenting on this last passage, says, "A man's sincerity and the clear transparency of his whole being must manifest themselves in his speech. It will be recognized there by those people who are sufficiently true and sincere to make out the real intention from the sound of the words they hear." [1] Those who are illumined by Christ live purely, for light produces all kinds of holiness (Eph 5:8–9). We can be sure of our knowledge of God and our union with him if we keep his word. One has Christ only if he behaves as Christ did. The holy person is begotten by the Lord (1 Jn 2:3–6, 29). By

---

[1] *The Gospel according to St. Matthew*, NTSR 1–2 (London: Burns and Oates, 1969), 1:231.

holy living or unholy living we can tell who are God's children and who are of the devil (1 Jn 3:10). The wicked simply do not know God (3 Jn 11).

This Johannine tradition is similar to the Jamesian: Mere earthly wisdom shows itself in unholy behavior: arrogance, jealousy, ambition, devilish animality, strife and all sorts of vile actions. Divine wisdom, on the other hand, is shown by humility, innocence, peace, docility, sincere kindliness (James 3:13–18).

False teachers especially show their errors in the laxity of their life-styles. Whereas the Spirit of God makes the man who possesses him strong, loving, wise (2 Tim 1:7), false teachers love themselves and money. They are arrogant, abusive, disobedient, licentious, lovers of pleasure rather than of God. They make a show of religion, and they are "always learning", yet never reach a knowledge of the truth. They actually oppose truth and falsify the faith. Yet their stupidity is evident for all to see (2 Tim 3:1–9). The late New Testament does not pull its punches on this subject. False teachers can go to extremes of conduct. They can excel in pride and disobedience, lust and revelry. Like waterless springs, they speak "empty bombast" while baiting their hooks with passion. Slaves to their sins, they have turned their backs on the holy law of the Lord Jesus (2 Pet 2:1–22).[2]

---

[2] See Alois Stoger, *The Second Epistle of Peter*, NTSR 22 (London: Burns and Oates, 1969), pp. 164–66, 168. If the reader is tempted to think that the biblical condemnations mentioned in this paragraph are excessive and thus may not be applied to our modern age, I suggest that he reflect upon Paul Johnson's historical study, *Intellectuals* (New York: Harper and Row, 1990). This volume documents in impeccable detail the moral depravity of a number of prominent writers who have articulated the very secularism that has begotten much of the licentious behavior of our day. Among the notorious characters Johnson examines are Rousseau, Marx, Ibsen, Tolstoy, Hemingway, Bertrand Russell, Sartre and Hellman. Yes, pride, lust,

Yet a problem remains. While virtue is a sign of authenticity, mentally ill people can sometimes present a picture of holiness that is mostly façade. Perhaps a perverse individual could also do it up to a point. K. V. Truhlar notes that we have here one reason why the policy of the Holy See in beatification processes is so stringent. He notes that a neurotic need for prestige and admiration can in subtle and unconscious ways give an appearance of striving for perfection that is more or less perverted by egoistic ambition.[3] This caution does not, of course, negate the validity of the biblical principle, but it does indicate the need for the specific signs we take up in our next sections. It indicates likewise the need for outer verification, the need that we have to escape our own subjectivity and be evaluated by others, especially by those whom God has placed in the Church for this precise purpose.

This general principle, authenticity begets goodness, becomes strikingly evident in advanced prayer. A valid experience of God produces goodness of itself. While God says little that is specific to most people, he says much by way of producing love, joy, peace, humility, purity in the soul. St. John of the Cross remarks that some of the divine touches are so deep and enriching that a single one of them could remove all of a person's imperfections and fill him with goodness.[4]

Specific biblical signs of authenticity are of three types: moral behavior, doctrinal criteria and communal criteria. Each of these types is a specification of the general principle: From their fruits you shall know them.

---

revelry, dishonesty, abusiveness do indeed beget intellectual errors—just as 2 Peter indicates.

[3] K. V. Truhlar, "Virtue, Heroic", NCE 14:709–10.

[4] *Ascent of Mount Carmel*, bk. 2, chap. 26, no. 6; p. 195.

Sign No. 1: God-Directedness

God is pure goodness because he is pure love. The man or woman led by his Spirit is likewise good and loving. We may say that a person may be confident of being led by the Holy Spirit only to the extent that he has matured in gospel goodness.

Moral behavior for the New Testament includes what we now call observance of the natural law, but it proceeds farther even to heights so sublime that unaided reason could not possibly suspect them. It proceeds into an utter God-immersion. The authentic person is a transformed person, the new creation. The first sign of this immersion, transformation, new creation that we will consider is the direction of all things to the Alpha and Omega.

Like iron filings close to a strong magnet, good people are drawn to God more or less irresistibly according to their degree of authenticity. The closer one is to the magnet, the greater the attracting force. This sign of the Spirit is best seen in Jesus' consuming passion to do the will of the Father. This was his meat and drink (Jn 4:34), his great absorption.

Authenticity and reality are two sides of one coin. This is why the saints are the most real people in existence. Masks, pretensions, style-slaveries, prestige seeking, myopic goals are all stripped off. The saint faces up to reality as it is, not as the world imagines it to be. Since every last shred of reality derives from the creative hand of God at every moment and is to be directed back to him as its ultimate purpose, the authentic person lives the Pauline "whether you eat or drink or do anything else, do all for the glory of God" (1 Cor 10:31).

An impulse received from God is necessarily an impulse

leading toward God. It could not be otherwise. The more a person is led by the Spirit, the more will his thoughts, aspirations, desires and decisions be orientated toward the Trinity. The more one's thoughts, aspirations, desires and decisions tend to a created object for itself, the more the inclination stems either from one's unredeemed nature or from the devil. St. John of the Cross writes:

> I should like to offer a norm for discerning when this gratification of the senses is beneficial and when not. Whenever a person, upon hearing music or other things, seeing agreeable objects, smelling sweet fragrances, or feeling the delight of certain tastes and delicate touches, immediately at the first movement directs his thought and the affection of his will to God, receiving more satisfaction in the thought of God than in the sensible object that caused it, and finds no gratification in the senses save for this motive, it is a sign that he is profiting by the senses and that the sensory part is a help to the spirit. The senses can then be used because the sensorial objects serve the purpose for which God created them: that He be more known and loved through them.[5]

To the spiritually immature, this may appear to be a grossly exaggerated ideal. That one would think of God immediately and chiefly in his perception of sense pleasures appears alien to most people's everyday experience. Admittedly it is alien to most people's experience. But all this proves is that unfortunately most people are spiritually immature—as Paul plainly told the Corinthians. The fully grown disciple finds far more delight in God than in anything of sense, and for him the latter leads to the former. Paul's ideal, "rejoice in the Lord always", is an expression of this truth.

God-centeredness is obviously a trait of a person full of the Holy Spirit (the last five words are favorites of Luke

---

[5] Ibid., bk. 3, chap. 24, no. 5; p. 255.

and Paul). This we accept easily enough in theory but not so easily in practice. It is, nonetheless, nothing more than keeping one's eye always on the Lord (Ps 25:15) and seeking him with all our hearts (Ps 119:10). St. John of the Cross is not exaggerating when he speaks of the advanced person as looking "for its Beloved in *all* things. In all its thoughts," says the saint, "it turns immediately to the Beloved: in all converse and business it at once speaks about the Beloved; when eating, sleeping, keeping vigil, or doing anything else, it centers all its care on the Beloved."[6]

Each of us has in this sign of the Spirit a solid criterion for judging his own genuineness. To what extent can I say that I do all for the glory of God, to please him: this particular type of recreation, this purchase of clothing, this pleasure trip? Is it really to please him or myself that I engage in this conversation, write this letter, read this book, watch this television program, submit this proposal, undertake this project, respond to this criticism, offer this other criticism? The indwelling Spirit leads to the Father and to nowhere else.

Sign No. 2: New Love

Love is an inner, invisible reality. As such it cannot be a sign of the Spirit's presence. But love sooner or later shows itself in action and thus becomes a visible signal of an invisible presence. This is what Jesus meant when he said that by our living of his new love all men would know that we are his disciples (Jn 13:34-35).

This new love is a singular reality. It is not merely propriety, cordiality, politeness. It surely is not a mere sexual

---

[6] *Dark Night of the Soul*, bk. 2, chap. 19, no. 2; p. 374.

response. The love the Holy Spirit pours out into our hearts, a love that discloses his presence (Rom 5:5), is a rare commodity in its complete external enfleshment. Agapē love is a gratuitous concern for the other for his own sake. It does not simply respond to goodness already present. It creates goodness where goodness was absent. We love our brother or sister with this new love when our caring for and about this person does not depend on whether we get something in return. So described, this love immediately appears as a light on a mountain.

People who live selflessly are readily seen as disciples of the Lord Jesus. Agapē love appears as a sign in that it is visibly patient and kind, not jealous, conceited, proud, irritable, ill-mannered or selfish (1 Cor 13:4–7). This love shares generously, works cheerfully, lives sincerely, cares warmly (Rom 12:8–10). It blesses those who persecute, never pays back evil with evil but conquers it with good (Rom 12:14, 17, 21). It is kind, tenderhearted and merciful in forgiveness even after the manner of the heavenly Father's mercy (Eph 4:32; Mt 5:44–48).

The first Johannine letter, a letter that deals heavily with discernment of truth from falsehood, includes this new love as one of the signs of authentic teachers in the late-first-century Church. The man who claims to have the truth, "to be in the light", and yet who hates his brother is still in darkness. It is the very darkness that has made him blind (2:9–11). The wealthy man who refuses to share his goods with a needy brother cannot be loving God: the visible nonsharing is a sign of the absence of inner love (3:17–18). Whoever loves his brother knows God because the love comes from God (4:7–8). All of this is also expressed in blunt terms: If a person affirms his love for God and yet hates his brother, he is a liar (4:20).

This sign of the Spirit needs to be translated into the nitty-gritty of daily life. We may ask how in modern life does the gospel love sign of authenticity actually appear? How does it aid us in detecting the finger of God in the welter of opinions, assertions, denials? We need not dwell on the obvious answers to these questions: warmth, care, sensitivity to feelings, sacrifice, interest. Important as these are, they are well known. Rather I shall touch on some signs of love (or its absence) not so readily seen in the authenticity–inauthenticity context. To illustrate our point we may take the admittedly difficult human problem of criticizing another person or his work or his policy. This criticism may be on the peer level of daily life or in the more unusual situation of the written word. It is not overly difficult to discover among critics who is being led by the Holy Spirit and who is not. It has been rightly noted that the sometimes necessary criticism in the Church heals no wound unless it consists in an example of greater love:

> [T]he critic without love resembles rather a man who scratches himself all the more furiously, the more fiercely he itches, a process which of course can only result in exacerbating and spreading the inflammation. The great saints were reformers of the Church but they were edifying reformers. Not all great reformers were saints, that is to say those who truly loved; many of them destroyed more than they built up. The fierce acids which today are dropped into the hearts of millions from the pulpit, from the press, radio, and television, or which are prescribed as medicine for man's enlightenment, in the interest of progress in accordance with the natural sciences and with the most recent exegesis, as medicine to enable man to turn (or indeed to convert himself) to the world, have hardly been brewed up by those who love the Lord.[7]

[7] Hans Urs von Balthasar, *Elucidations* (London: SPCK, 1975), p. 186.

One can picture Catherine of Siena disapproving of the papal presence in Avignon and yet at the same time profoundly loving the pope as her "Christ on earth". Her criticism had all the marks of the Spirit: made with reluctance, moderation, gentleness, accuracy and love. One need only compare this approach with its opposite: eagerness, exaggeration, harshness, bitterness. When one reads of theological disputes through the centuries (including our own), he sees clear examples of the two types of criticism. One has the marks of proceeding from God; it builds up in love. The other bears the brand of human pride; it cuts and erodes. The two kinds of phenomena are so common in daily life that illustration is superfluous.

Sign No. 3: Cross-Asceticism

Perhaps the supreme paradox of the incarnational economy is the paschal mystery, foolishness to men but the very wisdom of God. Pervading the entire New Testament (the old did not understand), this paradox is expressed in a rich variety.

The path of the Master (who *had* to suffer and thus enter his glory, Lk 24:26) becomes the pattern for the disciples. Persecution brings blessedness (Mt 5:10–12); a hard road leads to life (Mt 7:13–14); crucifixion begets resurrection (Rom 6:3–6); the dying seed brings forth abundant life (Jn 12:24); he who loses his life finds it (Mt 16:25); chastising one's body brings victory (1 Cor 9:24–27); the Father chastises those he loves (Rev 3:19); Paul possesses everything by having nothing (2 Cor 6:10); the degradation of the Cross is a saving power (1 Cor 1:18); being consigned to death is a showing of life (2 Cor 4:8–11); the humiliation of a crucifixion leads to a supreme exaltation (Phil 2:5–11); sacrifice leads to transfiguration (Phil 3:17–21). Only those who carry their cross daily and renounce everything they possess can be disciples of the Lord Jesus (Lk 9:23; 14:33).

Rightly motivated, suffering and asceticism are so much a mark of authenticity that the Christian is admonished not only to tolerate or be resigned to trials but to look on them as a happy privilege (James 1:2–4), to expect them, to rejoice in them as a blessing (1 Pet 1:6–7; 4:12–14). St. Paul claimed to know nothing but the crucified Christ (1 Cor 2:2), and he boasted in nothing but the Cross of Jesus by which the world was crucified to him and he to the world (Gal 6:14).

To the outsider all this is madness, but to those who have been called it is the power and wisdom of God himself (1 Cor 1:23–24). While it lies beyond our scope to develop the details of an ascetic life-style, we may offer a few brief reflections on why it is a sign of the Spirit's presence.

Sin obscures. So does selfishness. The cross purifies. All of us ordinary mortals are wounded, immersed in our own darkness. A healthy self-denial sensibly practiced and rightly motivated slowly lifts one out of his egoism, laziness, hedonistic inclinations. We are fitted to receive the clean light of the Spirit.

The saints invariably possessed a remarkable wisdom. Even the most simple of them were gifted with a penetration into reality and into the God of all reality that books and studies cannot produce. This penetrating gaze into the real was made possible by their prior purification. This must be at least part of the meaning of that mysterious saying of St. John of the Cross: "The purest suffering produces the purest understanding."[8] In another place the saint amplifies this idea when he remarks that "the purest suffering brings with it the purest and most intimate knowing, and consequently the purest and highest joy, because it is a knowing from further within."[9] One who lives the paschal mystery, life through death, lives more and more deeply and thus will see more and more penetratingly. Authenticity is begotten on the cross.

Suffering reduces us to our own ashes; it strips away egoism and makes love possible. A Scripture commentator can remark that "to be a 'tried' Christian or to experience the Spirit is one and the same. Trial disposes to a greater gift of the Spirit, for He now achieves by trial His work of liberation. Thus freed, the tried Christian knows how to discern, verify, 'try' everything."[10]

If adaptation to the modern world has actually meant settling for a more comfortable life, a rejection of the hard road and the narrow gate, it is no renewal at all. If updating in a religious congregation has consisted largely of mitigations, we have a clear sign of resistance to the Spirit of the living God. If the renewal of moral theology consistently means more pleasure and less sacrifice, it is no updating at all. It is a surrender to the world.

Sign No. 4: Frugality

This trait of authenticity is so foreign to most people's way of thinking that one feels a temptation not to discuss it.

---

[8] *Maxims and Counsels*, no. 48; p. 678.

[9] *Spiritual Canticle*, st. 36, no. 12; p. 549. Elsewhere John adds, "The endurance of darkness leads to great light" (Letter no. 1 to Madre Catalina de Jesus; p. 685).

[10] Jean Corbon, in DBT, p. 544.

Yet, startlingly enough, frugality represents not only a clear New Testament message but also a growing contemporary theme. As the earth's nonrenewable resources (oil, natural gas, iron, zinc and many others) slowly and irrevocably dwindle, a growing consensus in the academic community is calling for a fundamental change in our consumerist premises and practice. Whether we like it or no, the day is coming (indeed, its dawn is upon us) when we shall be forced to live more and more frugally. On the purely human plane, we see that individuals and nations that consume vastly more than their rightful share of the planet's resources are selfish and inauthentic, at least to the extent that they realize what they are doing.

But seeing things on the human plane is not enough. God's word has said a great deal about this matter long ago, a great deal that bears on authenticity and discernment. For the Johannine school, the very heart of genuineness is torn out of the person who does not share his wealth with the needy brother: he cannot be loving God who does not share his good things with the poor (1 Jn 3:17–18). Faith is dead in the man who passes by his hungry and ill-clothed brother or sister with a good wish but no material help (James 2:14–17). Genuine conversion is shown by the person who, having two tunics, gives one to the brother who has none (Lk 3:10–11).

The gospel is so strong on the relationship between poverty and authenticity that Jesus' teaching is met with shocked amazement. When the Master proclaims that the wealthy have greater difficulty in entering the kingdom of God than a camel in passing through the eye of a needle, the disciples are astonished. The Greek expression is strong: it means astonished, amazed, shocked, overwhelmed (Mk 10:23–27). Yet this is of one piece with others of his statements. They are in a blessed condition who are poor in spirit and in fact (Mt 5:3; Lk 6:20). The greatest man born of woman is not to be found in fine clothes (Mt 11:8). Cares, wealth and the pleasures of life stifle the word of God and prevent it from reaching maturity (Lk 8:14). Our life is not made secure by our possessions, and so we are invited to sell these possessions, give alms to the poor and follow the poor Lord (Lk 12:33).

There are two places in the New Testament where doctrinal teaching is greeted with ridiculing laughter, and both deal with material matters. One of these is Paul's speech on the resurrection of the body in Athens (Acts 17). The other is Jesus' teaching on the use of money: "The Pharisees, who loved money, heard all of this and laughed at him" (Lk 16:14). But Jesus had the last word, a withering word: "You are the very ones who pass yourselves off as virtuous in people's sight, but God knows your hearts. For what is thought highly of by men is loathsome in the sight of God" (Lk 16:15 JB). Love of money is a clear sign of inauthenticity. It is so inauthentic that God loathes the attitude. "The Lord grieves over the rich, because they find their consolation in the abundance of goods" (CCC 2547).

Hence they who are led by the Holy Spirit are content with necessities, with food and drink (1 Tim 6:7–8). They do not dress up for show with fine jewelry, elegant dresses and excessive care for the hair (1 Pet 3:3; 1 Tim 2:9–10). St. Paul is willing to be a fool for Christ: he is despised, hungry, thirsty, clothed in rags, a wandering pilgrim (1 Cor 4:10–13). After all, Jesus had told the Twelve that when they travel to proclaim the word, they are to take no bread, no money, no spare tunic, no beggar's bag. In all this they are simply imitating him who had no place to lay his head (Mt 8:20).

Frugality is not destitution, but it is frugality. When freely chosen in faith, it is a clear sign of the presence of the Holy Spirit, for it discloses a human heart set, not on things, but on the God of things. This did not escape the biblical prophet. "Isaiah (2:7) displays a Judah of unbridled, irresponsible luxury, a sensate society without thought for the spirit, divine or human. . . . Its wealth, therefore, Isaiah sees simply as another symptom of a towering human pride that has put its confidence in itself to the total disregard of the only God."[11]

The contemporary Church is reemphasizing her pilgrim poor character as a sign of her own renewed fidelity to him who became poor for us (2 Cor 8:9). Vatican Council II admonished bishops and priests to give their superfluous money to the works of the apostolate or to charity, and they are invited to embrace voluntary poverty as a way of life.[12] Everyone in the Church is told to give to the poor from their "substance" and not merely from superfluity.[13] The Liturgy of the Hours no less than three times in the Christmas office alone witnesses to the importance of frugality in the Church's life. One example: in the office for December 31, referring to Jesus' birth in circumstances of poverty, we pray, *"te rogamus, ut paupertas effulgeat in Ecclesia tua"*—"we ask that poverty may shine brilliantly in your Church."

The Church's mind regarding authenticity is displayed in fine detail in the men and women on whom she is willing to set the seal of her canonization. The saints are towering examples of the message of this volume from

---

[11] Bruce Vawter, *The Conscience of Israel* (New York: Sheed and Ward, 1961), p. 288.
[12] PO no. 17.
[13] GS nos. 69 and 88.

beginning to end. If anyone has listened to the Holy Spirit, they have. If anyone knows what the divine presence is like, they do. If anyone has the mind of the Lord God, they do. I know of no saint who lived a personally elegant life-style. Their genuineness shone through their selfless lives, their selfless frugality.

Sign No. 5: Uncluttered Freedom

God respects human freedom in more ways than one. He honors our native psychological liberty by allowing us to elect either the heights of the new creation or the depths of self-fashioned degradation. He desires to exalt us with the very summit of goodness and beauty, but he forces not the least speck of it on anyone. God wills the salvation of all, but he imposes it on no one.

One aspect of this respect can be seen in his waiting until we are freed from inner clutter before he gives his most exquisite gifts. Just as a flutist does not attempt to play an instrument clogged with foreign matter, so the Holy Spirit does not play in the stopped-up person. He works a transformation only in those who are transformable. He fills only the empty.

In the Old Testament, the desert, the wilderness, is a privileged place for meeting Yahweh. When Israel has been unfaithful by running after other lovers (idols), God seeks her conversion by sending a series of detaching privations. He makes her like an arid land, strips her naked, lays waste her vines and fig trees, recalls her grain, wine and oil and brings her feasts and joys to an end. Then Israel will be ready to return to its first lover. He is now ready to allure her into the wilderness and there speak to her heart (Hos 2:4–16).

It is significant that when Jesus wishes to explain why his word is sometimes heard with an initial receptivity but finally fails to reach maturity, he uses a suffocating verb to describe what happens. People, he says, are choked with the cares, the wealth and the pleasures of life, and they fail to come to fullness (Lk 8:14; Mt 13:22). A genuine disciple is not of this world just as Jesus was not of it (Jn 17:14–16). Anyone who makes himself a friend of this world becomes an enemy of God, an adulterer (James 4:4).[14] Lovers of pleasure may be always learning but they cannot reach the truth and so falsify the faith (2 Tim 3:4, 7–9).

Spiritual writers, therefore, are wholly in the biblical tradition when they insist that there is no holiness without the inner freedom of detachment. St. John of the Cross could assert that the hard road and the narrow gate are a sign of truth more important than miracles because they are so rooted in the word of God. In one of his letters the saint wrote, "If at any time, my son, someone—whether he be a superior or not—should try to persuade you of any lax doctrine, do not believe in it or embrace it; even though he might confirm it with miracles. But believe in and embrace more penance and detachment from all things, and do not seek Christ without the cross."[15]

---

[14] Since God's people is wedded to him in an indissoluble life of love, coming to terms with his enemy "is a form of adultery. . . . Anyone who does not respond to God's love with his whole heart, but keeps an eye out for other 'lovers', violates this loving union. Such a person wants another friend, the fallen world. . . . [There is] betrayal involved in every form of half-heartedness, in all 'leaning towards both sides', in all toying or dallying with the spirit of the world" (Otto Knoch, *The Epistle of St. James*, NTSR 21 [London: Burns and Oates, 1969], p. 209).

[15] Letter no. 22 to Juan de Santa Ana; p. 702.

8

DOCTRINAL CRITERIA

Important as moral behavior is as a sign of the Spirit's presence and activity, it is not enough. It must be complemented with a "clinging to the teaching of the apostles" (Acts 2:42). It is difficult in our present milieu of a cavalier attitude toward matters doctrinal to appreciate the repeated biblical insistence on sound doctrine. Whereas many of us tend to feel that as long as one means well it does not matter much what opinions he holds in religious affairs, for scriptural writers it mattered immensely what one held about God's revelation.

Sign No. 6: Sound Doctrine

For biblical men, authentic teaching was considered more important than miracles in distinguishing the true prophet from the false. The former could be known in that his teachings were in accord with received revelation (Dt 13:1–6).[1] The wrath of Yahweh breaks forth upon the heads of

---

[1] "Even in the OT, did not the Deuteronomist see in the doctrine preached by the prophets the authentic sign of their mission (Deut 13:2–6)? Thus it remains today" (Paul Beauchamp, in DBT 419). See also the article "Prophetism (in the Bible)", NCE 11:871.

the false prophets who were not sent by him but speak visions of their own imagination. It was promised that in the new dispensation God would place a new spirit, a new power in the hearts of his people, and from this inner source they would obey his outer word (Ezek 36:26f.; Jer 31:33). Jesus promised that this inner power, now known to be the Holy Spirit, would teach all that Jesus had taught (Jn 14:26). That man or woman cannot be of the Spirit who contradicts the truth the Lord has already committed to his Church. In this same spirit, St. Paul remarked at mid first century that no one can confess Jesus' lordship correctly without the aid of the Holy Spirit, and conversely no one who is speaking in the Spirit will ever utter a false statement about Jesus (1 Cor 12:3).

But as the first century wore on and false teachers began to proliferate, the New Testament writings became more and more vehement about the critical necessity of sound doctrine. Paul curses those who teach a gospel other than what has been taught (Gal 1:6–9).[2] The Colossians are admonished not to be deceived by any seductive philosophy or mere human opinions (Col 2:7–8). "The heretics at Colossae", observes Franz Mussner, "tried to pass their views off as a 'philosophy'; this was bound to make a good impression with certain people; it sounded as if it meant a higher form of wisdom and understanding."[3] Paul, on the contrary, appealed to the traditions handed down by the apostles. So it goes in any age. Those deviating from the gospel speak of their position in attractive, relevant-sounding terms. But Paul was on to this sort of tactic. The

[2] See Gerhard Schneider, *The Epistle to the Galatians*, NTSR 15 (London: Burns and Oates, 1969), p. 15, and Joseph A. Fitzmyer, in JBC 49:11.

[3] Franz Mussner, *The Epistle to the Colossians*, NTSR 17 (London: Sheed and Ward, 1971), p. 134. See also Joseph A. Grassi, in JBC 55:23.

author of Hebrews advises his readers not to be carried away by all sorts of strange teaching but rather to imitate the faith of their leaders (Heb 13:7–9).

The pastoral Letters abound in references to sound teaching as a crucial need toward the end of the first century. Timothy is to warn people against teaching false doctrines (1 Tim 1:3), and he is reminded that the Church of the living God is the pillar and safeguard of the truth (1 Tim 3:15). He is to guard the rich deposit of the faith with the aid of the indwelling Holy Spirit (2 Tim 1:14). This faith is to be handed on to trustworthy teachers and not to anyone at all (2 Tim 2:2). Then there follows a series of admonitions to correct error, even to the point of being persecuted, for there will come a day when people will not tolerate sound doctrine but will gather for themselves teachers who will tickle their ears with falsehood.

Titus receives the same message: Hold fast to the authentic tradition, encourage sound doctrine, refute those who contradict it (Titus 1:9; 2:1, 8). This pastoral insistence is of one piece with the rest of the Pauline emphasis on oneness of mind in doctrine and practice. One operates on thin ice if he sets the pastoral Letters against the other writings in the Pauline corpus. Raymond Brown notes that "there are first-rate Pauline scholars who still consider Paul as the author of the pastoral letters (in the broad biblical sense of 'author,' not necessarily in the current, restricted sense of 'writer'). And this is my own view", he adds. Brown remarks that even if further study should one day disclose that the pastorals are pseudepigraphical, their composer must have felt that

> their theology was close enough to Paul's to warrant the assumption of the Pauline mantle. A study of pseudepigrapha in the Bible seems to indicate that generally a pseudepi-

graphical work is attributed to an author because it is a continuation of his thought, style, or spirit, rather than because it is designed to correct his theology. Therefore we must proceed with care in drawing a sharp line of demarcation between Pauline theology and that of the Pastorals.[4]

It is right, therefore, to conclude with a prominent Pauline scholar that the "pastoral letters reveal the agonized concern of Paul and his collaborators over the rapid proliferation of errors in the churches they had founded."[5] And yet this concern is not confined to the Pauline churches, for we find it equally strong, perhaps at times even more vehement, in other late-first-century writings.

Throughout the First Letter of John, we find a repeated concern for the divisions in the Church that are caused by the false teachers. This is so much the case that it has been suggested that the principal theme in the Letter is discernment: How can the community members tell the true teacher from the false? This concern is expressed in different ways. The Letter itself is written that the recipients may be in union with those who articulate the community's faith (1:3). If they walk in light, they are united with one another (1:7). As long as they keep alive what they were taught in the beginning, they share in the trinitarian life of Father and Son (2:24). Of this text Bruce Vawter observes, "The safeguard of the true Christian who would avoid the dire consequences of this false teaching is to hold firmly to the teaching received through the apostolic preaching."[6] The true prophet can be distin-

[4] *New Testament Essays* (Milwaukee: Bruce Pub. Co., 1965), chap. 3.

[5] Lucien Cerfaux, *The Spiritual Journey of Saint Paul* (New York: Sheed and Ward, 1968), pp. 215–16. See also Martin Dibelius and Hans Conzelmann, *The Pastoral Epistles*, 4th ed. (Philadelphia: Fortress Press, 1972), p. 25.

[6] JBC 62:17. Luke reflects the same idea in Acts 2:42.

guished from the false by his doctrine on the Incarnation (4:2–3, 15; 5:1, 5).[7]

Though it is brief, the Second Letter of John shows the same concern. Noting that there are many "deceivers in the world", the author makes the point that only they who keep to what they were taught can have the Father and the Son with them (2 Jn 9–10). This sounds harsh to ecumenically tuned ears, but whatever else one may say of it, he must agree that correct doctrine was viewed as immensely important.[8] The Third Letter hints at the same theme: The author rejoices to hear that his "children" are living according to the truth (3 Jn 4). It is significant that the Book of Revelation concludes with a solemn warning that to anyone who adds to the prophecies in the book God will add all the plagues mentioned in it, while anyone who cuts away anything will be cut off from the tree of life and the holy city (Rev 22:18–19). The Letter of Jude exhorts the faithful to "fight hard" for their faith, and he warns that the false teachers are surely to be punished (Jude 3–19).[9] The same concern occurs in 2 Peter, where the author makes the point that, just as there were false prophets in the old dispensation, so there will be false teachers in the new. They introduce their own disruptive opinions and thus disown the Master and destroy themselves in the process (2 Pet 2:1–2).

It used to be the fashion to see the biblical prophets as opposed to ritualistic worship and therefore to official

[7] "Both in the OT and in the NT it is recognized that prophecy in order to be true must be consistent with known revelation" (Bruce Vawter, in JBC 62:22). See also Ralph Russell, in *A New Catholic Commentary on Holy Scripture* (Nashville: Nelson, 1975), p. 1260.

[8] See on this text: Vawter, in JBC 62:32.

[9] See the footnotes on this text in the *New American Bible*. W. J. Dalton gives interesting background in *New Catholic Commentary*, p. 1264.

sacramentalism. They were thus envisioned as radical innovators who could well be used as examples of resistance to official structures in the Church. This fashion has now withered to the point that most students of biblical prophecy hold that the prophets were traditionalists, not innovators. "In the last analysis, the criterion of true prophecy was its accord with known revelation. The touchstone of truth, therefore, has remained the same in the New Testament that it was in the Old; the words of 2 Tim 4:3f. apply equally well to the two revelations." [10]

Doctrinal fidelity as a mark of authenticity is sometimes an obvious sign, sometimes not so obvious. Flat contradiction of magisterial teaching is a clear indicator of inauthenticity, for the Holy Spirit does not lead the individual to reject the teaching of the very leaders he himself has established to protect the truth (Acts 20:28). While the genuine theologian attempts to develop and complement and unfold biblical and ecclesial teaching, he does not reject it. Scripture could not be more clear.

Not so clear are the more subtle signs of inauthenticity. One is the selective use of Scripture and magisterial teaching. One of the very best of the many positive results of postconciliar renewal is a reinsertion of our spiritual lives into the biblical word. Yet we would be deceived were we to conclude from this renewed interest in Scripture that everything in it is popular. One could list with no trouble at all a dozen themes—not single texts, but themes—that

[10] Bruce Vawter, *The Conscience of Israel* (New York: Sheed and Ward, 1961), p. 27. John L. McKenzie has captured the New Testament vehemence: "Those who teach and believe false doctrines are bereft of the truth (1 Tim 6:5), have swerved from the truth (2 Tim 2:18), oppose the truth (2 Tim 3:8), turn away from the truth (2 Tim 4:4), reject the truth (Tt 1:14)" (*Dictionary of the Bible* [New York: Macmillan Pub. Co., and London: Collier Macmillan, 1965]), p. 902.

are rarely mentioned (or mentioned favorably) in the literature. Among them are ascetical self-denial, hell, obedience to human leaders, superiority of virginity, factual frugality.

We find likewise the tendency to speak on religious topics with scarcely any effort to relate one's thinking with the biblical word. There are writers who weave their theology (it would not be untrue to say ideology) from their experience of life and from their grasp of psychology and/ or sociology. What we notice on the American side of the Atlantic is apparently obvious on the European side as well. William J. Philbin sees the tendency this way:

> In an age which was hailed as marking a return to the Scriptures many writings are appearing which are satisfied with a mere courtesy reference to a few texts from the inspired books. Theology nowadays is all too often regarded as under no obligation to consider how its speculation compares with the biblical evidence. Still less is any duty recognized to examine the teaching of a Church Magisterium whose function in regard to doctrine is so clearly laid down in Scripture.[11]

If one thinks that perhaps this is an exaggeration, I invite him to spend some time with current theological literature. He might look into my own field of specialization, religious life, and see how seldom writers make careful studies of the biblical evidence for what they are propounding. Responsible theologians and teachers do not operate in this manner.

---

[11] In Paul Surlis, ed., *Faith: Its Nature and Meaning* (Dublin: Gill and Macmillan, 1972), p. 161.

Sign No. 7: At Odds with the Prevailing Spirit of the World

God is not popular. Not the real God. He has never been popular, and he is not popular today. One who is caught up in the enthusiasm of thoroughgoing conversion is forever astonished and crushed that the majority of men and women neither acclaim the undiluted gospel nor seem to make extraordinary efforts to live it. They who proclaim the word either in speech or in print are forever surprised when many remain indifferent to the message or reject it outright. But the surprise is mistaken.

Part of the message itself is that the message will not be favorably received by the majority. It is a hard road and a narrow gate that lead to life, and only a few find it (Mt 7:13–14). From Amos 5:15, where the remnant idea occurs for the first time in Scripture, through to Matthew 22:14, where we read that the elect are few, we are repeatedly reminded that the faithful will be a little flock. It is true that the gospel will be proclaimed in the whole world, that the mustard seed is to grow into a large tree, but the message will always be at odds with the prevailing spirit of the world. Jesus does not speak on an earthly plane (Jn 3:31), and so many leave him. Paul proclaims a wisdom not of this age because the wisdom of the world he considers absurdity with God (1 Cor 2:6; 3:19). The genuine disciples are the salt of the earth (Mt 5:13; Lk 14:34–35), an image that likewise suggests both smallness and great diversity from the generality. The authentic word is wheat mingled with the straw of error, and the prophet who proclaims it is like a burning fire and a hammer shattering rocks (Jer 23:28–29).

We ought not to be surprised that the world hates the faithful disciples. Yet strangely enough we are surprised.

We expect the Church's teaching to be acceptable to the majority. We tend not to hear the many times the New Testament proclaims the world's hatred for the authentic proclamation and for those who announce it. The very first of the New Testament canonical writings refers to the persecution of the faith as being widespread and much to be expected (1 Th 2:14–16; 3:3–4). Jesus himself had said that his followers would be blessed when men hate and ostracize and insult them (Lk 6:22). Even members of one's own family will reject, persecute and kill the faithful person: "All will hate you because of me" (Lk 21:16–17). John's Gospel is every bit as explicit: The world hates the disciples because it has hated Jesus before them, for neither he nor they belong to the world and what it stands for (Jn 15:18–19; 17:14–16).

This pattern is normal, and it continues on to the end of the first century. The faithful are advised not to be surprised if the world hates them (1 Jn 3:13), and they hear that they should rejoice when they are insulted for the sake of Christ (1 Pet 4:12–14). Anyone who makes himself a friend of the world thereby becomes an enemy of God (James 4:4). He, on the other hand, who is faithful to Christ is sure to be persecuted (2 Tim 3:12). The two dispensations can be summarized by the question Stephen addressed to his own murderers: "Was there ever any prophet whom your fathers did not persecute?" (Acts 7:52).

Rejection as a sign of authenticity ranges all the way from indifference to the message to the shedding of blood because of it. The pages of the New Testament provide abundant examples of teaching that the hostile element in the world flatly rejects: a frugal life-style embraced gladly and with love . . . the narrow gate and the hard road . . . a demanding chastity in matters sexual . . . the avoidance of pleasure seeking as though it were an end . . . the reality of hell . . . the superiority of virginal dedication to God . . . hungering after holiness . . . continual prayer . . . avoidance of elaborate hairdressing and fine clothing . . . humility and obedience . . . long periods of prayer in solitude. The true prophet disturbs consciences.[12] And most people do not like to be disturbed.

The world can be so ill in its intellectual and moral life that it unwittingly assumes as normal what a few moments' careful consideration easily shows to be a widespread disease. If one lives with omnipresent sickness long enough, he begins to assume that it is normal, especially if he has little contact with healthy people. An American psychiatrist has pointed out that there is no little illness in our Western culture's preoccupation with genital sexuality. He considers it no exaggeration "to say that a majority of marriages must be defined as states of obsessive-compulsive preoccupation with genital sex. Such a married state is by definition characterized by a lack or diminished degree of freedom in sexual matters because of an obsession with sexual thoughts, images, and desires." This compulsion, he notes, spills over only too easily into pre- and extramarital activities. In this

[12] On the other hand, the false prophet is popular because he soothes the consciences of the wayward with his easygoing teaching. Of Micah 3:9–12, we read that "the vicars of Bray, too, have reacted in their perennially predictable way, obediently furnishing texts as required to bless whatever deeds their masters care to have clothed with respectability. The instruction (*torah*) given by the priests is no longer recognizable as the moral law of Israel's God; it is a *torah* shaped and accommodated to the aspirations of ruthless men who demand value for their money. The professional prophets are likewise at their old stand, purveying oracles that disturb no conscience but countenance with divine approval the conduct of a people that can do no wrong" (Vawter, *Conscience of Israel*, pp. 147–48).

doctor's judgment, the number of persons with a healthy, integrated sexuality is exceeded in our society by those who are ill in this area of their lives. Thus we find moralists who reject Catholic principles and proclaim "as a moral norm what is only attainable by the psychologically immature person and thereby implying that the latter is incapable of growing as yet toward the ideal of perfection". In this ill atmosphere there then arises "a false need for contraceptive techniques, legalized abortions, and euthanasia".[13] An ill world slowly takes its illness as its normal state and so rejects the healthy life pattern set out by God. Health is bound to be at odds with illness.

So it is in the history of God's people that the genuine prophet is persecuted, even killed. Because the people scorn the word of the Lord (Jer 6:10), they logically enough scorn him who proclaims it. Jeremiah complains that he has become an object of laughter, mockery, derision, reproach. He wrestles with the Lord to get out from under this outrage (Jer 20:7–8). Hosea complains that the prophet has been considered a fool and a madman (Hos 9:7).[14] Though each age is surprised when it happens anew, happen it will: authenticity is not at home in this world.[15] The Church is necessarily a stranger, a nomad, unwelcome on the face of the earth (Heb 11:13–16; 1 Pet 2:11).

[13] Conrad W. Baars, M.D., *A Priest for All Seasons* (Chicago: Franciscan Herald Press, 1972), pp. 8–15.

[14] "Hosea's words are general: Israel has rejected not one but the whole line of prophets, the natural, hostile response of the guilty to the reprover" (Denis J. McCarthy, in JBC 15:25; see also Paul Beauchamp, in DBT 415).

[15] SC no. 2.

9

COMMUNAL CRITERIA

God did not disclose his revelation to private individuals either in the old or in the new dispensations. He proclaimed it to a people, to a community, to his *qahal*, his *ekklesia* (Heb 1:1–3). Especially by the Word made flesh did he draw a new people together, close among themselves, close to himself.

There is consequently no authenticity that is merely private. True enough, each of us must one day face the utterly Alone ourselves alone. True enough, as unique persons we must spend much time in solitary prayer with the unique One. But it is also true that we shall account for our life in community, our life of prayer with our sisters and brothers, our life of sharing our persons, our life of feeding, clothing, visiting the Lord himself in the persons of his least ones. We receive the healing word and sacraments of the Lord Jesus in the context of his Church: "He who hears you, hears me."

The *ekklesia* is one universal community. Yet it embraces thousands of subcommunities woven together into one unity: parishes, dioceses, religious congregations, noncanonical groups of diverse types. The first three of these are themselves made up of many lesser groupings:

families, priests living a common life, local communities of religious congregations.

Given the fraternal character of God's people, the question arises: Are there evangelical marks by which a community can itself be known as possessing the Holy Spirit, as being authentic as a community?

Sign No. 8: Unity

The answer is yes, a resounding yes, a surprising yes: "With me in them and you in me, may they be so completely one that the world will realize that it was you who sent me" (Jn 17:23).

Though many of us have read this sentence dozens of times, it is likely that few have taken it seriously. *Complete* unity! A unity patterned after the absolutely perfect oneness of the Trinity!

Even allowing for the due and vast differences between things divine and human, the ideal is so remarkable that it is humanly impossible. Yet this very unity is a primordial mark of the presence of the Spirit in a group. As a matter of fact, this sign of the Holy Spirit's presence is one of the most radical of biblical teachings on discernment. The Spirit does betray his presence and activity in a community, and the New Testament makes it plain that this presence and activity are proved by a tangible miracle, a humanly impossible oneness: "so completely one that the world will realize that it was you who sent me".

No less than four remarkable points are made in this one verse. The first is that the unity is so perfect and complete that nothing is lacking to it. The second is that the unity is patterned on nothing less than the unbreakable oneness of Father, Son and Spirit. Thirdly, it flows from the indwelling presence of the Lord within the community. And lastly, it is a miraculous unity, for from it the world can conclude that the Incarnation has taken place—nothing but the finger of God could cause this phenomenon: "that they may be one as we are one".

What this unity excludes is spelled out elsewhere in the New Testament. Whereas we tend to take divisions and factions as part of life and therefore to be expected (hence we insist on toleration and "live and let live"), the New Testament would have none of this dilution. While there was room for a healthy complementary diversity rooted in a shared vision of the essentials, there was no room at all for dissensions and factions. St. Paul is so set against the divisions in the Corinthian church that it is his first item of business. He spends several chapters on the subject. The first sentence of his discussion is a pleading for a oneness, a perfect oneness of mind (1 Cor 1:10). Later on in the same letter, he withers the Corinthians in telling them they are spiritually immature, worldly. And how does he know that some at least are not living the gospel? Their divisions are the telltale sign, for the Spirit brings unity (1 Cor 3:1–3; CCC 790–91). These same factions likewise are an impediment to the worthy celebration of the Eucharist (1 Cor 11:17–34). Since the Eucharist makes the many to be one (1 Cor 10:16–17), a community that lacks unity must be resisting the Eucharist itself.

A similar point is made in 1 Timothy 2:8: Prayer is to happen in the context of communal peace and harmony. This is also why sound doctrine is important: Diverse teachings cause contention and mistrust (1 Tim 6:3–5).[1] James' analysis of divisions and contention is similar:

[1] "Paul deliberately refers to the teaching of the church and the Lord's words in one breath. The teaching of the church is the Lord's teaching"

Selfish desires are the basic root (James 4:1). Otto Knoch notes that serious tension, jealousy and quarreling are a sure sign that motives are purely selfish.[2]

But it was Jesus himself who began the insistence on unity in community as a signal of authenticity. Not only did he require complete unity, but he had earlier warned that a house divided against itself could not survive (Mt 12:25). History is a continuing witness to the validity of the warning. The world community breaks up with an unending series of wars and balances of power. A growing percentage of marriages end in the tearing experience of divorce. Polarized religious congregations wither on the vine of the Church.

The apostolic Church of the first century looked upon communal love and harmony as a sign of the presence of the Holy Spirit. St. Paul had admonished the Galatians that factions and divisions were numbered among the sins of idolatry, sexual irresponsibility, orgies and sorcery. A community beset with wrangling, factions and feuds did not have the Spirit with it. The reason was that the Holy Spirit brings love, joy, peace and harmony (Gal 5:18–22). St. Luke was of the same mind. When he came to summarize the state of the prospering churches in Judea, Galilee and Samaria, he noted that they were "filled with the consolation of the Holy Spirit" (Acts 9:31).

The theology behind this sign of the Spirit is both simple and sensible, even though the consequences can be frightening. Why is communal unity a sign of communal authenticity? People who are open to the light and love of

---

(Joseph Reuss, *The First Epistle to Timothy*, NTSR 19 [London: Burns and Oates, 1969], p. 75).

[2] *The Epistle of St. James*, NTSR 21 (London: Burns and Oates, 1969), p. 206.

God will necessarily be of one mind and heart (Acts
4:32)—they drink a shared vision from the one Spirit of
unity. People who are divided in mind and heart (some, if
not all of them) must be closed to this drinking.

Sign No. 9: Obedience Freely Given

The New Testament abounds in this sign of detecting the
inner workings of the Holy Spirit in the individual and in
the community. The person full of God obeys his superiors. The community full of the Spirit obeys its leaders in
the Church at large. Our problem here is superabun-
dance, how not to overwhelm the reader with citations
and yet to offer enough to achieve full impact.

The biblical thought may be summarized by saying that
he is obeying the invisible God who obeys the visible representative of God. Or, to put the matter in more technical terms, he practices unmediated obedience to God who
practices mediated obedience to human authority. Or,
still differently, we may say that he is under illusion who
believes himself to be following the inner inspirations of
the Holy Spirit but refuses to fulfill the outer directives of
his rightful human superior.

In both Testaments God identifies himself with his representatives, and that is why cooperation with them is a
sure sign of compliance with God's will. This is not to be
understood as though the representative necessarily has
some privileged knowledge of the "content" of the divine
mind. Rather it means that God wills that his representatives be obeyed (unless, obviously, they command something clearly sinful).

The identification of God with his representatives has
its roots in the Old Testament. The Lord puts his own

words into the mouth of his prophet, so that if anyone does not listen to the prophet, he is not listening to the Lord (Dt 18:18–19). When the Israelites grumble against Moses and Aaron, the Lord God considers the complaints to be lodged against himself. Therefore they are severely to be punished (Nb 14:2, 27, 35–37; 16:11). From the day the fathers left Egypt, Yahweh untiringly sent them his prophets, but they did not obey *him* when *they* spoke (Jer 7:25–26).[3]

Jesus continues this thought pattern: "He who hears you, hears me; he who rejects you, rejects me; and he who rejects me, rejects him who sent me" (Lk 10:16).[4] This is understood so realistically that when people do not receive or listen to the disciples, the disciples are to leave the house or town and shake the dust from their feet. On judgment day it will be easier for Sodom and Gomorrah than for that town (Mt 10:14–15). Jesus so identifies with the decisions of those he sends that whatever Peter and the other apostles bind or loose on earth is bound or loosed by God himself (Mt 16:19; 18:18).[5]

The apostolic Church of the first century understood herself to be speaking in the divine name, so that they who

---

[3] F. W. Young, a Protestant writer, is correct in speaking of this pattern almost as a law: "When God speaks, he does so through his chosen representatives, a patriarch or judge (Judg. 2:17), prophet, priest (Deut 17:12), King (2 Kings 10:6). . . . God fulfills his purposes in and through human beings" (*The Interpreter's Dictionary of the Bible* (New York: Abingdon Press, 1962), 3:580–81.

[4] For commentary on this text, see Alois Stoger, *The Gospel according to St. Luke*, NTSR 5–6 (London: Burns and Oates, 1969), 1:198; and Augustine Cardinal Bea, in *A New Catholic Commentary on Holy Scripture* (Nashville: Nelson, 1975), pp. 4–8. The Johannine rendition of this identification is found in John 13:20.

[5] Vatican Council II understood this power to refer both to doctrinal and to disciplinary decisions. See LG no. 22.

proclaimed the good news did it in the power of the Holy Spirit (1 Pet 1:12).[6] Hence the faithful are listening to this Spirit when they listen to the heralds of the Word.

In a little, compact treatise on discernment appearing toward the end of the first century, obedience to leaders is presented as the final sign of the true teacher. "It is not every spirit, my dear people, that you can trust; test them, to see if they come from God; there are many false prophets, now, in the world. . . . Those who know God listen to us; those who are not of God refuse to listen to us. This is how we can tell the spirit of truth from the spirit of falsehood" (1 Jn 4:1, 6 JB).[7] Rudolf Schnackenburg finds this same criterion in Mark's Gospel (Mk 3:22–27): "For the young church," he observes, "it became a criterion of the 'discernment of spirits' whether one accepted her confession of Jesus or not."[8]

If obedience to leaders is a sign of authenticity, we would expect admonitions to this obedience in the pages of the New Testament. Our expectation is not disappointed either at the chronological beginning or at the end. St. Paul urges the brothers to hold fast to the tradi-

[6] See Benedikt Schwank, *The First Epistle of Peter*, NTSR 22 (London: Burns and Oates, 1969), p. 44.

[7] Even if one were to agree with Bultmann that "us" refers to the community, the leaders are understood, for they articulate the faith of the community and are charged in the New Testament with proclaiming it. Bultmann himself implies this when he adds that "the difference between the spirit of truth and the spirit of deception becomes discernible in whether the proclaimed word is heard or not" (Rudolf Bultmann, *The Johannine Epistles* [Philadelphia: Fortress Press, 1973], p. 64). Joseph Pegon is on target when he writes of this text that "St. John adds that the experience of the Spirit has to be the same as the teaching received from the Apostles" (NCE 2:560).

[8] Rudolf Schnackenburg, *The Gospel according to St. Mark*, NTSR 3–4 (London: Sheed and Ward, 1971), 1:63–64; italics in the original.

tions they received from him either by word of mouth or by letter (2 Th 2:15). He expresses confidence that they will continue to do whatever he enjoins (2 Th 3:4). He commands them to avoid anyone who departs from the tradition or does not obey his injunctions (2 Th 3:6, 14–15). The apostle tests the Corinthians to learn whether they are obedient in all matters (2 Cor 2:9). In addition to these practical expectations, there are the many straight-out directives to practice obedience (Heb 13:17; 1 Pet 5:5; Col 3:18, 20, 22–23; Eph 5:21, 24; 6:1–2, 5–7).[9]

The obediential sign of authenticity is so striking in the New Testament that, contrary to all expectations, we learn that a divine manifestation is itself to be submitted to a human approval. As I note elsewhere, Paul, with his un-doubted direct commission from the risen *Kyrios*, is told to submit his enterprise to the "leading men" in Jerusalem (Gal 2:1–10). In the course of history the unrooted enthu-siast attempts to do just the opposite: in his judgment it is he who approves, or more commonly disapproves, of the structural element in the Church. The same Paul in no uncertain terms makes it clear to the Galatians that they are not to accept a teaching from a messenger from heaven if it contradicts what they have received from the human leaders in the Church (Gal 1:6–9). Commenting on Mark 6:11, Schnackenburg notes that "he who does not receive the messengers of God (i.e., men sent) excludes himself from salvation, faces the judgment of God, and is con-victed by his witnesses. As a sign that the messengers have nothing in common with such places they are to shake even the dust off their feet."[10]

---

[9] For further commentary, see Henry Wansbrough, in *New Catholic Commentary*, p. 1079, and Schwank, *First Epistle of Peter*, p. 102.

[10] Schnackenburg, *Gospel according to St. Mark*, 1:103. See also 2 Pet 2:10.

This obedience is rendered, not because the one in authority is wiser, better, more genial or more experienced. He may be all of these (or he may be none of them), but they are not the reason. A participation in the divine authority, a deputation to an office, is the reason. Even the hypocritical scribes and Pharisees, who were to receive a tongue-lashing from the Lord, were to be obeyed because they occupied the chair of Moses (Mt 23:1–3). Contrary to a common misconception, Jesus was not one who broke the law, even if he had the mission to replace it and bring it to perfection. What he did violently oppose were the merely human traditions and interpretations that led men to violate the genuine law and reject the word of God himself (Mt 23:13–39). He kept the law himself and said it was to be fulfilled to the letter, to the smallest part of the letter (Mt 5:17–18).[11]

For St. Paul, authority is to be obeyed because all of it derives from God (Rom 13:1–2). We find the same teaching toward the end of the first century, namely, every human institution is to be obeyed because God commissions it and he wills obedience to it (1 Pet 2:13–15). St. John of the Cross repeatedly applies this principle to direct communications supposedly from God: "He [God] does not want the soul to believe only by itself the communications it thinks are of divine origin, nor that anyone be assured or confirmed in them without the Church or her ministers."[12] This is why in the Ignatian scheme of things the

---

[11] On this point, see Theodore Stylianopoulos, "Tradition in the New Testament", *The Greek Orthodox Theological Review* 15 (spring 1970): 7–21; Paul Beauchamp, in DBT 415; John L. McKenzie, *Dictionary of the Bible* (New York: Macmillan Pub. Co., and London: Collier Macmillan, 1972), p. 500.

[12] *Ascent of Mount Carmel*, bk. 2, chap. 22, no. 11; p. 183. The saint speaks of this at length in nos. 8 and 9.

manner of communal discernment changed after the Society of Jesus had a superior general who would appoint other superiors. Of this, Gervais Dumeige writes that "there would still be community discernment, but in other forms. The superior would make the decisions, but with the intervention of the entire community, or part of it, to help him in his discernment." [13]

Why is mediated obedience a sign of detecting the mind of God? Not because we need to suppose that the authority figure has a personal pipeline to the Holy Spirit and in that sense can reveal the divine will to us. No, the person in charge has the same problem the rest of us have: to be so converted and innerly good that the word of the Lord can penetrate into his mind and heart. The reasons lie elsewhere.

We speak of discernment of spirits in the plural. Those of us who are not yet ready for canonization are frequently and hiddenly and subtly led by our own spirits of a hundred types: of vanity, avarice, ease, comfort, reputation-seeking, lust, laziness, pleasure-seeking. We are only too ready to think that our proposals and desires are nobly inspired, and we are prepared at the drop of a hat to offer a list of lofty reasons why we propose what we propose. Obedience tends to bring an element of objectivity into the swampland of our ignoble inclinations. And they who believe themselves to have few ignoble inclinations are far more likely to be led by them than they who do know it.

A second reason why mediated obedience is a sign of discernment is that God does not contradict himself. He does permit unworthy, yes, and we may admit it, sometimes stupid men and women to be appointed to office.

[13] "Jesuit 'Deliberation' and Discernment", *The Way*, supplement no. 20 (autumn 1973): 61.

But still he does not contradict himself. Supposing that the officeholder himself is obedient to the Holy See, God who works within the hearts of the faithful (Rom 8:14) also governs through the structural element in his Church (Acts 20:28). He alone is the assurance that the latter will not ultimately destroy or harm the former. And history bears out the correctness of this conclusion.

10

CONVERSION AND
THE ATTAINMENT OF TRUTH

Be converted . . . this is the only way to discover the will of God
and know the perfect thing to do.—Rom 12:2

The popular model for reaching truth is the research-experimentation model. One leaves ignorance behind and pushes forward the frontiers of knowledge through patient study and hard-nosed criticism. Palpable evidence is the ultimate criterion.

It goes without saying that there is a great deal of truth in this popular model, but it is only part of the truth. Research and study are the avenues leading to a certain level of knowledge, not to all levels. We may distinguish two types of knowing: one is particular, specific, thing-centered, while the other is fundamental, deep, ultimate, person-centered. Examples of the first are the molecular structure of water, the sum of the angles of a triangle equaling 180 degrees, the location of Chile in South America and the defeat of Napoleon at Waterloo. Examples of the second are moral decisions, the ultimate purpose of life, the thirst of men for happiness and the quest for God.

The research-study model for the attainment of truth is effective for the first level of knowing. A proud, avaricious, lustful person can through sheer study reach an extensive knowledge of things. He can learn precious little about persons, nothing about God—nothing, that is, that transcends the mere data level of books and lectures. Deep, ultimate, person-centered knowledge is achieved through love, genuine love. And love is achieved only through conversion from an opacity resulting from the original fall. Biblical conversion is an about-face, not a mere improvement. *Metanoia* is a fundamental change of mentality, a reversal of outlook. Evangelical conversion envisions no mere level of strategic error, routine mistaken judgments. It runs deeply. In Johannine terms, it is the difference between light and darkness (Jn 3:19; 1 Jn 2:8), offspring of God or of the devil (1 Jn 3:10), life and death (1 Jn 3:14). In Matthean terms it is the difference between one road that leads to perdition and another that leads to life (Mt 7:13–14). In Pauline patterns it is the cleavage between flesh and Spirit, worldliness and godliness (Rom 8:5–13; 12:1–2).

Some Curious Problems

Unvarnished truth is not popular—which is one way of putting the reason for Jesus' death. We must face in this chapter some odd facts, and we must ask some questions not often asked.

The first question bears on the non-intellectual elements involved in intellectual conclusions. Two people can examine exactly the same evidence and come up with opposite conclusions. For example, two men can reflect on the innate human refusal to accept death and evil as the final commentary on the human situation. Both agree that this refusal is a fact, but they draw opposite conclusions. One, an atheist, concludes with Nietzsche that this refusal represents man's weakness, a weakness that leads him to postulate another world of truth and goodness. The other, a theist, sees in this refusal man's strength, namely, a trace of the divine in the human heart, a yearning that stretches into the very realm of the infinite. There is more in this disagreement than intellect. Both men have made basic choices that serve as unexpressed premises. When they look at evidence, they see through their free choices. How and why does this happen?

A second curious problem concerns the extraordinary tenacity with which most people cling to their opinions in the areas of morality, politics and religion (areas, by the way, that bear directly on quality and type of lifestyle). Why do so many men and women resolutely refuse to accept cogent evidence against their positions? For decades scientists have been discussing and disagreeing as to how to explain the macromutations that many of them feel have taken place in an evolutionary process. One general thrust explains it by chance (which, of course, by definition is not an explanation but only an assertion), while the other postulates a directing cause. Some years ago the scientist Lecomte du Nouy wrote the book *Human Destiny*, and in it he showed how mathematically impossible it would be, given the magnitude of the universe and the time it has existed, for even one protein molecule to be formed by chance collisions of atoms. As far as I can ascertain, that vast challenge of du Nouy's contention has been met with a wall of silence. The silence was recently underlined by one who reissued the unmet challenge:

> There is a book, *Human Destiny* by Lecomte du Nouy, which has lain dormant for over 20 years and may yet, like an unexploded bomb, blow sky high this tepid discussion of the existence of God. . . . Mr. du Nouy's arithmetic shows con-

clusively that there has not been enough time for these processes, by a frightening number of exponents of 10, for them to have taken place by any such fortuitous events. The scientist, in any pragmatic reconstruction of such events, is forced to include in his equation a directing, leading force quite outside his usual thinking.[1]

Why this vast resistance to *conclusive* evidence? It cannot be basically an intellectual matter. It must be largely mixed with will. Yet it is not only scientists who can refuse evidence. Theologians can and do the same. The contraception controversy is a case in point. The arguments of those who support the popular position have been devastatingly destroyed, and the conclusions drawn from the popular position are now so well known and widely practiced (pre- and extramarital and homosexual relations) that almost no one can be unaware of them. Yet once again there is the vast silence and the tenacious clinging.

A third odd question: Why do those responding to a critique of their position often reply selectively or not at all? I have found both in my own writing experience (including private correspondence) and in that of others as well that often a response is not forthcoming at all, or if one is offered, it significantly omits discussing the most telling elements in the book or article or letter. If we suppose that the one criticized is intelligent, it is difficult to avoid the conclusion that he has no response. But if this is the case, why does he not admit it? Is this honesty or evasion? If it is the latter, what is the reason?

A further problem: Why, despite the recent advances both in biblical and theological research (for example, into

[1] David H. Dodd, "Letters from Readers", *National Observer*, October 20, 1973, p. 12.

the Petrine-papal question), is ecumenical progress so slow? We may take for granted the obvious answers to this question: centuries of polemic background, lack of information at the grass-roots level, sinful faults on both sides during the sixteenth-century Reformation. But these explanations are not adequate. Something deeper is involved. The objective biblical and patristic data are in the public record. Why are they sometimes read so differently or even rejected?

The Biblical Explanation

The typical theologian or moralist seems to assume in his discussions of disagreements that most if not all the obscurities and cleavages are due to insufficient data and/or inadequacies of analysis. He assumes that at least in theory full discussion should yield agreement. He operates under the unspoken law that no one is ever to suggest that free will has something to do with the reason why theologians and ethicists hold what they hold. The taboo is so strong that almost no one dares to study the problem and the suggestion. Yet there is probably no more basic ecumenical question than this one.

When we turn to the biblical discussions of religious-moral disagreements and rejections, we find a world almost totally at odds with what I have just described in the preceding paragraph. It is so at odds that our main concern is that the investigator may reject it out of hand without giving it the careful thought it deserves. What is the biblical explanation? We will take it step by step.

Sin causes inner darkness. The first step is that sin causes darkness. We find that deceit or wrongdoing is a very road of darkness (Prov 2:12–15), that wisdom neither enters nor remains in a sinful person (Wis 1:4), that the godless do not see the light of justice; they never know the way of the Lord (Wis 5:6–7). The *Catechism of the Catholic Church* states that "sin is an offense against reason, truth and right conscience" (CCC 1849). Those who defy the precepts of the Most High live in gloom and darkness (Ps 107:10–11). Even more, the wicked do not understand the meaning of holiness, while those who serve God understand everything (Prov 28:5). They who trust God grasp the truth (Wis 3:9), and they who love wisdom readily find and see her (Wis 6:12–13). The Lord shines for the upright as a lamp shines in a dark room (Ps 112:4), but he does not shine for the evil. He shows his face, his presence to those who turn to him with complete abandon and with no dishonest rationalizing (Tob 13:6). Because the good person has interiorized the transforming word of God, he is endowed with perception (Ps 119:104).

The connection between quality of living and quality of knowing is not merely factual; it is also causal. Sin darkens the mind, brings obscurity. After a lengthy description of life as the godless see it (Wis 1:16–2:20), the sage concludes that such were the thoughts of the evil. They erred because their very wickedness blinded them (Wis 2:21). Earlier we read that when the chosen people grew fat, gross and restive, sacrificed to demons and forgot the God who fathered them, they became short of sight, a nation of no understanding (Dt 32:15–20, 28).

St. Paul was of the same mind. Not only does the man of the flesh, the worldly person, fail to understand the things of the Spirit; he *cannot* understand them (1 Cor 2:14). Knowing goodness and truth are simply beyond his capacity. Worldliness impedes detection of religious and moral truth just as nausea impedes the appreciation of good food. St. John of the Cross remarked that they who lack a sound palate seek other tastes and cannot savor the spirit and life of God's words. The divine message actually becomes distasteful to them.[2] Elsewhere St. Paul asserts that they who live the philosophy of eating, drinking and making merry do not know God at all (1 Cor 15:33–34). The god of this world blinds the eyes of the unbelievers and prevents them from seeing the light shed by the good news (2 Cor 4:4). We read in John's Gospel that everyone who does wrong hates and avoids the light—it exposes his evil life-style (Jn 3:20). Yet it is characteristic of the unconverted that he assumes his own superior insight, and he pities what he considers the pathetic blindness of the spiritual man.

Not only are the unconverted in error. They do not even grasp what causes their error. Their way, says the sage, is like darkness, and they do not know over what they stumble (Prov 4:19). The history of theology teems with illustrations of this truth. While some people hold to their errors with more or less conscious ill will, others fit the biblical explanation: their sight is so deeply wounded that they are not capable of suspecting either the error itself or the reasons for it.

Frighteningly, a positive closing of one's mind to God is possible. The prophet speaks of those who refuse to listen, who stubbornly turn their backs and stop up their ears, who make their hearts diamond-hard against the truth. They are set not to hear the message as spoken through the Lord's representatives, the prophets (Zech 7:11–12). St. Mark ascribes the disciples' lack of understanding simply to the fact that their minds were closed (Mk 6:52).

---

[2] *Living Flame of Love*, st. 1, no. 5; p. 581.

When biblical writers, therefore, come to explain why some persons detect the mind of God and others do not, they do not offer the explanation that the former are more intelligent or have studied more deeply. They locate the difference in the presence or absence of moral goodness and in the presence or absence of a desire for the truth. The root of knowing God is the human will as it expresses itself in moral choices and style of life.

Scripture makes little provision for people erring in good faith about the basic reality of the divine self-disclosure. There is no evidence for the thought that they who reject the true prophets or Jesus' representatives do so in good conscience. On the contrary, they are roundly condemned as rejecting God himself (Lk 10:16) and worthy of anathemas (Gal 1:6–9). The New Testament is remarkably intolerant of people entertaining private views regarding doctrine and morality contrary to the teaching of the *ekklesia*'s leaders.

The will, root of error. It is a short step from saying that sin causes inner darkness to saying that one chooses basic religious error. He may do it either explicitly by a perverse choice, or he may do it implicitly by choosing a life-style incompatible with truth. Nowhere does Scripture suggest that men and women fail to find God because they have a low intelligence quotient, because they are dull of wit. Invariably and in diverse ways the deepest explanation is located in choice.

For the prophets, the House of Israel is a set of rebels, stubborn and obstinate. They refuse to listen either to Yahweh or to his representatives (Ezek 2:5–9). They are a people who have no taste for God's word. They cannot listen because their ears are uncircumcised, their hearts are evil (Jer 6:10; 7:24). The prophetic explanation of a refusal to accept God's teaching is that people choose to stop their ears. They make their hearts adamant (Zech 7:11–12). It is not because the listeners lack intelligence or because the prophet is unskilled in speech. It is because the people have freely chosen not to accept the divine instruction.

New Testament writers are of the same mind. Repentance of an evil life comes before an acceptance of the good news proclaimed by Jesus (Mk 1:15). The preaching of the disciples confronts the world with a fundamental choice, not an academic debating possibility. The choice is a matter of free will, a choice of salvation or damnation (Lk 10:9–15). The Gospel does not seem to envision the likelihood that a rejection of the good news can happen in good faith. The converted person accepts the word of Jesus' representatives, while the unconverted does not (Lk 10:16).

Even miracles do not prevent the willed refusal to repent (Mt 11:20). So deeply is basic religious-moral error rooted in the will that not even a resurrection from the dead convinces one who does not want to believe (Lk 16:31; cf. also Jn 15:24). People who refuse to listen to Jesus' disciples will undergo a hard judgment on the last day, a judgment more severe than that on Sodom and Gomorrah. As a sign against this culpable rejection, the disciples are to shake the dust from their feet as they leave the sinful house or town (Mt 10:14–15). Prostitutes can get into Jesus' kingdom more easily than those who refuse to believe him (Mt 21:31–32). Those who are open to his message find that it makes a deep impression on them (Mt 22:33).

The Johannine literature repeatedly returns to this theme. If anyone is ready to do God's will, he will know the source of Jesus' teaching—a good will opens to the perception of truth (Jn 7:17). Nothing Jesus says penetrates the minds of the Jewish leaders because their deeds are deeds they learned from their father, the devil (Jn 8:37–38). The Lord explicitly asks why they cannot (not simply: do not) accept his teaching. His answer: They cannot understand his language because they live as their father, the devil, wants them to live (Jn 8:43–44). They refuse to listen because they are not God's children. The good person, God's child, does listen to his teaching (Jn 8:47).

This same thought occurs under the shepherd-sheep image. The Jews do not believe because they are not Jesus' sheep, that is, they have not chosen to belong to him, whereas those who have so willed do listen to his voice (Jn 10:26–27). Those who are on the side of truth listen to him (Jn 18:37). The rejection of Jesus and his representatives is not due to misinformation or mere mistaken judgment— it is itself a sin for which there is no excuse (Jn 15:20–22, 24; cf. Jn 16:9 and 1 Jn 3:1). The rejecting will is bad basically because there is no love of God in it. Men look for approval from one another, not from God. Therefore they cannot believe (Jn 5:42–44).

St. Luke tells us that people who resist the gospel are stubborn; they have "pagan hearts and pagan ears" (Acts 7:51). Lionel Swain notes that the expression used in Scripture, hardness of heart (for example, Eph 4:18), suggests "the mysteriously culpable character of the Gentile's ignorance".[3] St. Paul asserts that depraved people keep the truth imprisoned in their very wickedness (Rom 1:18). In one of the very earliest New Testament writings we find a powerful, awesome explanation of religious error. When one hears the word of God, two choices lie open before

---

[3] *A New Catholic Commentary on Holy Scripture* (Nashville: Nelson, 1975), pp. 1188–89.

him: accept it, or choose wickedness. They who are destined to ruin have not opened their hearts to saving truth. Because of this free choice, God sends upon them "a perverse spirit which leads them to give credence to falsehood" (2 Th 2:10–12). This is frightening. The heretic is perverted, sinful, self-condemned (Titus 3:10–11). Thus the faithful are to be on their guard lest they be "led astray by the error of the evil" (2 Pet 3:17).

One need hardly observe that all this is highly offensive to modern ears. Many of us both assume and say that divisions among the great world religions and within Christendom itself are largely due to lack of information and the faults of churchmen past and present. We assume that almost everyone is in good faith, that few are sinning against evidence and the light that God gives. While there is no doubt that current conditions are somewhat different from those in the old dispensation and during the first century after Christ, yet the basic human confrontation with his message remains fundamentally unchanged. Yes or no to Jesus continues to be a willed choice.

Contemporary Scripture scholars are of one mind on this matter. I will cite one example and then offer other similar references in a footnote. Commenting on Ephesians 4:17–19 and applying Paul's reference to the pagans "holding down the truth in their wickedness" (Rom 1:18), Max Zerwick remarks that the "evil will is therefore the root of the matter. They could have known better, they did know better, but they did not *wish* to know, and hence they are holding down the truth." [4] This biblical

---

[4] Max Zerwick, *The Epistle to the Ephesians*, NTSR 16 (London: Burns and Oates, 1969), p. 117; italics are Zerwick's. See also J. Terence Forestell, regarding 2 Thessalonians 2:12, in JBC 48:33; Wolfgang Trilling, *The Gospel Gospel according to St. Matthew*, NTSR 1–2 (London: Burns and Oates,

analysis is reflected in our own century by Alexander Solzhenitsyn when he remarked, "We do not err because truth is difficult to see. It is visible at a glance. We err because this is more comfortable."

The teaching of psychologists and ethicists on unconscious motivation is relevant to this problem. It is widely admitted that the best of us bring to our actions and omissions motives of which we are quite unaware. There is not the least reason to suppose that we are not profoundly motivated on the unconscious level regarding our religious decisions. This obviously includes what we want to see and what we do not want to see, what we care to investigate and what we do not care to investigate, whom we choose to read and whom we do not choose to read.

From the point of view of experience of sin and sanctity, error and truth, it would be difficult to find a more suitable witness to this problem than St. Augustine. No one to my knowledge has better described what it is to be immersed in sins (both those of pride and those of aberrant sexuality) and at the same time to be immeshed in errors of intellect. His *Confessions* is an eloquent testimony to the darkness caused by sin and the enlightenment brought about through holiness. He experienced both.

Several times in the *City of God* Augustine touches on the interworkings of will and intellect in the matter of

1969), 2:11, regarding Matthew 13:13–15; Alois Stoger, *The Gospel according to St. Luke*, NTSR 5–6 (London: Burns and Oates, 1969), 1:196–97, regarding Luke 10:8–12; A. Theissen and P. Byrne, in *New Catholic Commentary*, p. 1133, regarding Romans 10:19–21; Tomas O'Curraoin, in *New Catholic Commentary*, p. 1167, regarding 2 Corinthians 4:3–4; Robert Javelet, *The Gospel Paradox* (New York: Herder and Herder, 1966), p. 204, regarding Luke 16:31; John L. McKenzie, "Know, Knowledge", *Dictionary of the Bible* (New York: Macmillan Pub. Co., and London: Collier Macmillan, 1972), pp. 486–87.

being in religious and moral error. His analyses are both interesting and of one piece with those of Scripture, even when he is not adverting to the divine word. He notes that a clear thinker should not have to use many words in correcting error except for the fact that there is in the human family a major and prevalent illness, a perverse obstinacy that prevents people from accepting clearly seen facts even when they are confronted with ample evidence (bk. 2, chap. 1). Later on in the work he remarks that everyone knows that neither his first five books (in the *City of God*) nor any five hundred books are sufficient to silence pertinacity. This disease is never cured, the saint adds, not because the doctor is inept, but because the sufferer is incurable (bk. 6, chap. 1). When people are burdened and broken by their sins, their minds are blinded by a love for darkness and iniquity (bk. 7, chap. 31). The language is almost Johannine; the thought surely is.

Conversion, condition of light. The conclusion is clear: One attains full religious and moral truth only when he has done an about-face, undergone a moral revolution, a conversion. The Lord God pours wisdom into the innermost being of the repentant sinner. He gives new sounds of joy and gladness to him, creates in him a renewed and steadfast spirit, bestows his holy power, a willing spirit (Ps 51:8–14). When the wicked person turns from his sins and does good, he again begins to live (Ezek 33:19). Jesus relates in one breath the reformation of life and belief in the gospel: "Repent and believe in the Good News" (Mk 1:15). It is significant that an about-face in morals precedes acceptance of the gospel. Conversion of life (at least a will to change life-styles) is the condition for readiness for the kingdom (Mt 4:17). Peter proclaims flatly to his audience that repentance is the prior condition for receiving the Holy Spirit (Acts 2:38). A season of refreshment sent by the Lord is a consequence of a turning from sin (Acts 3:19–20). One comes to know God by loving. The person without love simply does not know God, because God is love (1 Jn 4:7–8).

This notion of conversion as a condition for perception is reflected also in the Orthodox tradition. Gregory of Sinai asserts that "the understanding of truth is given to those who have become participants in truth, who have tasted it through living."[5] The introduction to the Russian translation of the *Philokalia* contains the same idea: "Only those can understand such notes as are following the path of that kind of life."[6] This is why the wisdom of this world is foolishness to God (1 Cor 3:19). It finds its goal in the finite order, an order that is utterly incapable of reaching the divine. To choose this is to render oneself incapable of attaining the supreme good.

Both with the earlier prophets and with Jesus himself a massive rejection greets the proclamation of God's love and truth. There seems to lie imbedded in the human heart a "mysterious obduracy" (Wolfgang Trilling) that resists the Old Testament prophets, the very teaching of Jesus and the continued proclamation of his Church. Not much has changed in twenty-five centuries. Isaiah declared and Jesus quoted him: The nation is dull and they have shut their eyes, lest they be converted and healed (Is 6:9–10; Mt 13:14–15).

Theological analysis. While the biblical explanation of religious error is neither doubtful nor obscure, we must candidly admit that it is not widely shared by our contem-

[5] In *Writings from the Philokalia on Prayer of the Heart*, trans. E. Kadloubovsky and G. E. H. Palmer (London: Faber and Faber, 1951), p. 42.
[6] Ibid., p. 14.

poraries, at least not by those who write or speak in a popular vein. As we have already noted, it is commonly supposed that those who reject Christ and his Church do so in good faith and for at least apparently good reasons. This common supposition invites further exploration.

We can distinguish two main concepts of conversion to God and to his truth, that is, two main suppositions of how it happens psychologically that a person turns to the Lord. One concept emphasizes the intellectual element, the other stresses the volitional. The psychological steps in the conversion process are quite opposite in the two analyses.

In the intellectual emphasis, the first step in the conversion process is a seeing of truth with the mind (for example, grasping the evidence for God's existence). The second step is accepting the truth one sees. The third is a sustained effort to live a good moral life in conformity with what one sees. The final step is the attainment of God, the end of the process. In this explanation the free will does operate, but the burden of the process is an understanding of truth.

In the volitional emphasis, the first step in the conversion event is a fundamental free choice, a willed Yes to the absolute mystery that surrounds one—one chooses to affirm the human situation and the Author of it. The second step is an attempt to live a good moral life in accord with the basic affirmation of God. The last is the seeing of a relatively full truth about God and about all else as related to him. In this explanation one's intellect does operate (there is no freedom without mind), but the main element is the willed affirmation.

What is the relevance of these two explanations? Does it make a practical difference which one we favor?

When one embraces the intellectualist view of conversion, he explains basic religious and moral differences among philosophers, theologians and common people on the basis of some persons seeing relevant evidence more deeply or studying more thoroughly. He would argue that the more persons who disagree listen to one another, the more deeply they study, the more ecumenical groups can meet in a cordial atmosphere, the more will differences disappear.

This explanation is attractive and does contain some truth. Cordial relations and competent scholarship do tend to unite. And there are intellectual elements in religious and moral controversies. But nonetheless the intellectualist explanation does no more than explain surface disagreements. It scarcely touches the deep ones and therefore does not explain all the facts. People do disagree who see exactly the same evidence and study with the same degrees of competence and thoroughness. Scholarship does not dissipate worldviews. It does not dissipate basic *choices* that all normal adults make. Bernard Lonergan, noting that dialectic deals with conflict, goes on to observe that

> there are differences that will be eliminated by uncovering fresh data. . . . But beyond these there are fundamental conflicts stemming from an explicit or implicit cognitional theory, an ethical stance, a religious outlook. They profoundly modify one's mentality. They are to be overcome only through an intellectual, moral, religious conversion. The function of dialectic will be to bring such conflicts to light.[7]

We disagree widely in moral and religious matters because we have fundamentally different cognitional, ethical

---

[7] *Method in Theology* (New York: Herder and Herder, 1972), p. 235.

and religious premises, premises that we choose, not prove. If these premises do not correspond to reality (and contradictory premises cannot all correspond to what is— some must be wrong), neither will the conclusions that flow logically from them. To achieve basic truth there must be a conversion from false to true premises. One does not have to be particularly perceptive to see that if a basic outlook or stance is erroneous, so will the consequences that follow consistently from it. Or, to change the image, one is going to see reality according to the color of the glasses he is wearing.

Intellectual Conversion

We all have cognitional premises. Even the most unsophisticated among us function in human life according to cognitional presuppositions we have absorbed in one way or another. We rarely attempt to prove them. For example, some people hold that human knowledge does not transcend the sense level. For these people there is no such thing as immaterial, spiritual ways of knowing. Others hold that the human person knows both in material (sense) ways and in immaterial (intellectual) ways. When these two groups look at the same identical data (for example, extrasensory perception, the miracles at Lourdes, the Gospel accounts of Jesus' divinity), the first group necessarily rejects the conclusions even before it looks into the alleged phenomena. It must reject them. Its premises are narrow and do not admit the conclusions. The second group can hold itself open before the evidences and, if satisfied with them, can assent.

Other cognitional premises bear on the relative importance of the types of knowing: experience, reason, revelation and authority. Some people judge an assertion or doctrine according to "whether it fits my experience of life", and they care little about reasoning processes or statements of authority. Other people are impressed more deeply by the other types of knowing. In each specific case or problem, not all these differing emphases can be right. Someone is out of touch with reality and needs a cognitional conversion. This is why theologians can know equally well the data from Scripture, patristic literature, magisterial teaching and the signs of the times and still disagree in their basic positions. John Courtney Murray could observe regarding repeated attacks on the caricatures of natural law that "those who dislike the doctrine, for one reason or another, seem forever to be at work, as it were, burying the wrong corpse. . . . In this respect, of course, the nineteenth century exhibited those extensive powers of learned misunderstanding which it possessed to an astonishing degree."[8] This astonishing power of learned misunderstanding may also partially explain why scholars so seldom change their basic positions even after sustaining devastating criticism.

Moral Conversion

Intellectual stance does not stand alone. It influences and is influenced by moral and religious options, especially the basic options.

Once again it must be pointed out that we all have fundamental moral premises that we have freely chosen. Not 1 percent of a population try to prove their validity or even reflect on their existence. But exist they do.

[8] *We Hold These Truths* (New York: Doubleday, Image Edition), p. 283.

What are some of these ethical premises? They deal with what people consider good or better. Some people so live their lives that prestige is valued far above honest humility, or pleasure before sacrifice, or pragmatic expedience before objective principle, or self-fulfillment before concern for one's neighbor, or diversity in community before unity of mind and heart. Other persons operate on premises quite the opposite. When, therefore, particular moral questions arise, it cannot be a surprise that the two groups of people disagree about what is good and what is evil.

Ethical truth can be consistently attained only after one has undergone an ethical conversion, and whether or not he has undergone this conversion is going to color also his positions in other areas of thought. Yet another question needs to be raised.

Why does sin obscure perception of religious and moral truth? This question supposes a distinction. There are neutral factual truths that do not affect the quality of our lives, our life-styles. That two plus two equals four or the theoretical information that the sun is approximately eight hundred thousand miles in diameter has scant influence on my moral choices. But there are other value truths that are anything but neutral apropos of my life-style. That God exists or that the Catholic Church speaks with his authority or that contraception is wrong are judgments that profoundly affect people's life-style. The main reason we differ so little in chemistry and physics and so much in religion and morality is that the former are neutral fields, whereas the latter are not. The reason is not that the former have evidential proofs, and the latter do not.

We like to think that our religious, moral and political choices are exclusively the result of clear, cool, intellectual insights. A moment's reflection shows this to be untrue.

Clear, cool intellects can examine the very same evidence in these fields and come up with opposite conclusions for practice. This fact points to another, namely, that basic decisions in religion, morality and politics are made on a level of our being deeper than our conscious reflections and motivations. We have made fundamental choices that color the specific evidence we see so that we see them in one way rather than another.

These fundamental determining choices are precisely that, choices. They are either real or unreal, true or false. They correspond to what is, or they do not. They are authentic or inauthentic.

How we decide specific questions depends on how we have already decided our basic positions. These latter powerfully influence how we react to God's existence, the Church, Mary, the papacy, sexual morality and a host of other questions.

Piet Fransen has pointed out that sin is the only radical threat to the purity of our interpretation of divine experience because it damages the very roots of the experience. Sin is fundamentally a refusal of light and love. It likewise damages our thinking about ultimate realities.

Religious Conversion

By religious stance I mean one's basic position apropos of God. Do I affirm God's existence, or do I deny it? If I affirm, is he really my supreme value? Is he my deepest love? Or am I? Does he play a conscious, vibrant, ever-present part in my life, or do I have him somewhere on the periphery? Am I or am I not a man of prayer?

That the answers one gives to these questions (not merely in theory but in life) profoundly affect one's theological and moral thinking I take to be obvious on a moment's reflection. On the atheistic premise, Albert Camus was consistent in finding human existence absurd. On the theistic premise, St. Paul was consistent in finding joy always and everywhere. On St. Francis' premises, factual frugality makes perfect sense. On Hobbes' premises, it makes no sense. On Jesus' premises, Catholic sexual morality (including virginity) makes eminent sense. On materialistic premises, it does not.

One may object at this point that our analysis lays too great a stress on the subjectivity of the thinker and too little on the objectivity of the theological enterprise. Bernard Lonergan has been criticized for shifting the focus of theological method from object to subject with the result that we must turn our attention from the subject matter of theology to an analysis of the mind of the theologian. This shift of focus includes the posing of the problem of the theologian's personal relationship to God. And so it has been asked why the intention, even the state of grace or nonstate of grace, of the theologian should be given a priority over the stuff of the theological enterprise. This involves a shift from the objective argument and text to some sort of intuitive encounter with the author of the argument and text.[9] This would seem an odd way to do theology.

It may be said in response that even if Lonergan may have laid too great an emphasis on the subjective mind of the theologian, it is by no means apparent that this vitiates his insights into the cruciality of conversion for the doing of sound theology. One can go to the opposite extreme of seeing a human science (whether it be anthro-

[9] See Fergus Kerr. O.P., "Objections to Lonergan's Method", *New Blackfriars*, July 1975, pp. 305–16; specifically at 308–9.

pology, sociology, psychology, philosophy or theology) as so objective a matter of out-there evidence that he supposes all investigators approach, weigh and sift this evidence as completely cool, detached observers—which they clearly do not. To pose the problem of the theologian's personal relationship to God is not entirely to subjectivize his work. It is simply to reckon with the plain fact that two persons may look at exactly the same argument or data and come out with opposite reactions. Something besides objectivity is at work.

We now see easily why St. Paul insisted that the only way to attain a knowledge of God's perfect will is to undergo a conversion from worldliness to holiness (Rom 12:1–2). The Father reveals his wisdom only to the humble (Mt 11:25–26), and it takes no minor conversion to be rid of pride. The arrogant may amass vast stores of data-knowledge, but this is a far cry from attaining the divine mind about what to do with the data. Those who penetrate into the mind of the Lord are those who love, are obedient and detached, hold on to sound doctrine and listen to their leaders (Jn 13:35; Heb 13:17; Lk 14:33; 2 Tim 4:1–4; Titus 1:9; Lk 10:16; 1 Jn 4:6). The conversion is a revolution.

Pope Paul VI was quite correct, therefore, when in the Holy Year of 1975, a year dedicated to reconciliation, he called for the conversion of those dissenting from the Magisterium of the Church. The call may have shocked and offended those to whom it was addressed, but it is beyond debate that some of the rejections of magisterial teaching were and are so deep that to look on them in any other way would be wishful thinking. Those rejections have the earmarks of almost every sign of the false prophet.

Fullness of Conversion

Conversion is susceptible of degrees, and so therefore is the attainment of the divine mind. Sensitivity to the Spirit becomes so entire in the transforming union that not only does one do what God desires, but even the first movements of one's feelings, inclinations, thoughts and desires are directed toward him. The person at this stage of advanced prayer is so entirely immersed in God and under his sway that even before his free will intervenes, even without advertence, his first movements are instantly inclined toward God.

Full conversion is saintliness. And saints are few. After remarking that madness is someone else's eccentric behavior and that no one of us is entirely and perfectly healthy, G. K. Chesterton went on to say that if there were

> to appear in the world a perfectly sane man he would certainly be locked up. The terrible simplicity with which he would walk over our minor morbidities, our sulky vanities and malicious self-righteousness; the elephantine innocence with which he would ignore our fictions of civilizations— these would make him a thing more desolating and inscrutable than a thunderbolt or a beast of prey. It may be that the great prophets who appeared to mankind as mad were in reality raving with an impotent sanity.[10]

Such a perfectly sane man did appear. His name was Jesus. He was not only locked up. He was put to death. Time has not changed basic things. Most people do not tolerate the truth. They either ignore it, reject it, persecute it or kill it.

---

[10] *Lunacy and Letters* (New York: Sheed and Ward, 1958), p. 10.

Curious Problems Revisited

We may return to the questions we posed at the beginning of this chapter. Why and how do men and women of equivalent competencies look at the same evidence and come up with opposite conclusions? In matters that affect life-style, our wills have a great deal to do with our conclusions. Basic free choices of cognitional, ethical and religious presuppositions profoundly affect more surface decisions and positions. This fact is seldom mentioned as an explanation for differences among the churches or even among members of the same church. I may cite a happy exception. Recently a priest was reviewing a book written by another priest. Toward the end of his evaluation the reviewer wrote: "Our differences seem to lie in our different theological stances. I would describe mine as relational and his as intellectual; mine as incarnational, his as transcendent. My view of God and man would be dynamic or evolutionary, his static and unchanging. We have different worldviews that would give us different interpretations of the first page of the daily paper." [11]

I am not sure that the description of the differences is entirely fair to the book's author, but I am sure that the first and last sentences ring true. If two Catholic priests can have different worldviews, it would be most interesting if those worldviews were spelled out and their underlying premises brought to light. It would be most interesting if the polarized segments in the Church would state openly for all to hear and to read what their basic cognitional, ethical and religious assumptions really are. No little fog would be dissipated.

[11] Dennis J. Geaney, reviewing *Listen Prophets!*, by George A. Maloney, in *National Catholic Reporter*, June 6, 1975, p. 11.

To illustrate how refreshing all this would be, I may be permitted a brief flight of fancy. We may suppose that someone would put together a technically competent questionnaire whose items would deal with fundamental (not surface) cognitional, ethical, religious stances. This questionnaire would be given to the five hundred men and women who speak and write most commonly on matters theological, ethical, ecumenical, religious. These people would freely consent to respond in all honesty and to have the results published.

What would be refreshing? We would then easily understand why we have a far right and a far left . . . why polarized religious congregations are bleeding and dying . . . why contending factions in the Church do not budge an inch from their positions . . . why dissenters dissent and the hierarchy holds fast . . . why faddish movements appear and die . . . why some accept Catholic teaching on sexual morality and others do not . . . why some emphasize freedom and others stress authority . . . why some accept the papacy and others do not . . . why conclusive evidence brought against a position is either ignored or evaded . . . why ecumenical progress is so slow.

Let me say this in an unfanciful way. While we need continued study and research in matters ecclesial, we need even more humility and conversion and love. Too many of us may not have yet reached the realization that just perhaps we have sinful premises we neither admit nor regret. We may be out of touch with God's mind because we have basic cognitional, ethical and religious stances that block him from our sight. We may cry out against the errors and sins of the "rest of men" as did the Pharisees but fail to pray as the publican, "O God, be merciful to me, a sinner." Rather than examine our own consciences, we have to a wearying degree been examining the hierarchy's conscience. Speaking of this phenomenon, Giacomo Biffi (in *Le Cinquième Évangile*) wryly remarked that we can with this procedure joyously and humbly recognize each evening the Church's sinfulness and then make the firm proposal for the morrow that to the extent of our capacity we shall change her. Thus we serenely sleep the sleep of the just.

PART FOUR

VERIFICATION AND IMPLICATIONS

11

VERIFICATION: INNER AND OUTER

From the superficial point of view, it would appear that
the question of discerning the Holy Spirit is largely if not
exclusively a matter of man detecting God in the deep recesses of his being. We would not be far from the mark in
supposing that when most people engage in a discerning
process either in community or in private prayer, they
look upon themselves as doing something private, that is,
without much if any relationship to the institutional
Church. I have my doubts that this perception is ever true.
I am sure that it is often at best a half-truth, sometimes a
complete distortion.

The Spirit Operates Incarnationally

The reader who has persevered thus far into our discussion probably suspects well enough what I mean. God
takes our humanity much more seriously than we do.
People who think themselves the most liberal and progressive are often the least so. And the subject of this volume provides a suitable example. Those who reject the
institutional elements in the Church would be horrified
to learn that they are angelists. They have opted for a

Christianity of the spirit alone. They have chosen not to take human bodyliness seriously on the deep levels of existence. Yes, they take more than a passing notice of sexuality and eating and drinking, but when it comes to the human side of the Church, they choose to turn their gaze to the angels.

Christ and St. Paul and the whole New Testament community were hardheadedly human. They knew better than we (because they were more holy than many of us) of human weaknesses and failings, but they could not imagine an invisible Church of Christ. In more than a theoretical way, the disciples knew they were not angels, and they could not have dreamed of the *ekklesia* of the bodily risen *Kyrios* lacking effective institutional elements. Graphically St. Paul reminds the overseer-bishops of Ephesus that it was the Holy Spirit himself who established them in office, and it is through these human instruments that the Spirit will deal with "fierce wolves" who invade the flock (Acts 20:28–31).[1] The apostle goes so far as to say that anyone who objects to his teaching is not objecting to a human authority but to God himself, who gives us his Holy Spirit (1 Th 4:8). The Thessalonians are to foster the "greatest respect and affection" for their leaders (1 Th 5:12–13). All sorts of gifts from the spirit are given to the authorities in the Church: apostleship, prophecy, teaching, leading (Eph 4:11–13). Regarding this last text, Max Zerwick notes that we would expect from 4:7 that the gifts here would be graces; but instead they are the bearers of

---

[1] Regarding this text, a recent commentary remarks, "the reason for their appointment does not lie in their own decision or in the will of the community, though both these play a part in it, but in the Holy Spirit who has made them 'guardians.' And this gives their office a special value" (Josef Kurzinger, *The Acts of the Apostles*, NTSR 10–11 [London: Burns and Oates, 1969–71], 2:101).

grace. The man plus his office is a gift of grace, whether he be an apostle, a prophet, a pastor, a teacher. "And then, after 'to each one of us' (4:7), one would expect that Paul would speak of *all the members* of the body of Christ. But now the only ones who appear are those whom we call the authorities in the Church. *They* are primarily the 'gifts' of the exalted Christ. Primarily, indeed, but then they bring the others in their train."[2]

This bodily-structural element in the *ekklesia* comes out in many ways in the New Testament: Jesus sends men into the world, and they speak with his own authority so that those who listen to these representatives listen to him (Mt 28:16–20; Lk 10:16) . . . the leaders in the Church test the authenticity of her members (Rev 2:2; pastorals, passim) . . . all are to obey their spiritual leaders (1 Pet 5:5; Heb 13:17) . . . they who disobey are inauthentic, not from God (1 Cor 14:37–38; 1 Jn 4:6) . . . even a supposed messenger from heaven may not contradict what the human leaders have taught (Gal 1:6-9) . . . the presiding officer in the local church has all sorts of duties in the areas of teaching and governing (1 and 2 Tim and Titus) . . . the Holy Spirit is with them in the performance of these duties (2 Tim 1:6, 14).

Although we do not find the same degree of organization in the first-century *ekklesia* that we find in that of the twentieth century (it would be amazing if we did), we do find a plurality of functions that are clearly governmental. The leaders teach and proclaim the word (1 Tim 3:2; 4:13, 16; 5:7, 17; 6:2; 2 Tim 1:8; 2:2, 14, 24; 4:1–5; Titus 1:9; 2:1–10, 15; 3:1–8; Acts 20:28). They pray for the sick and heal them (James 5:14–15). They correct aberrations and

[2] Max Zerwick, *The Epistle to the Ephesians*, NTSR 16 (London: Burns and Oates, 1969), pp. 109–10.

errors and faults (1 Tim 5:20; 6:17; 2 Tim 2:25; 4:1-5; Titus 1:9-14; 2:15). They govern the ecclesial community, the Church of God (1 Tim 3:5; 2 Tim 1:14; Acts 20:28; 1 Pet 5:1–4). These superiors are said to be God's representatives, and their authority is not to be questioned (Titus 1:7; 2:15). The faithful are told in plain language to obey these leaders and do as they say (Heb 13:17; 1 Pet 5:5).

All this makes it easy to agree with Raymond Brown when he says that "the constant insistence throughout the New Testament that those who are placed over others must humbly serve speaks eloquently for the thesis that the concept of a Church without human authority would have been strange at any period of New Testament ecclesiology."[3]

Yet at the same time the early *ekklesia* could not imagine herself lacking the invisible dynamism of the Spirit giving light and love and power and joy. They knew of the inner elements in their community not only because they had the word of the Lord for them but also because they experienced the very presence of their giver. There seems to be no pressing need in this present chapter to detail at length the New Testament account of the inner activity of the Holy Spirit in the *ekklesia*. We may note in passing that he enlightens the disciples with all truth (Jn 14:26; 16:13) . . . he gives inner wisdom, power and love (Eph 1:17-19; Rom 5:5) . . . he brings to the community harmony, love, joy, patience (Gal 5:22) . . . he bestows inner freedom, and he leads the faithful to the Father (2 Cor 3:17; Rom 8:14) . . . he is the fountain of charisms in the body of the Church (1 Cor 12:4-11).

---

[3] *New Testament Essays* (Milwaukee: Bruce Pub. Co., 1965), p. 69. See also John L. McKenzie, "Church", *Dictionary of the Bible* (New York: Macmillan Pub. Co., and London: Collier Macmillan, 1972), pp. 134, 136.

In the popular mind there probably still lingers the idea previously proposed by some writers that in the mid-first-century churches there was some sort of theoretical as well as practical opposition between charismatic gifts and structural elements. Recent studies show this notion to be mistaken. St. Paul writes vigorously to the divided Corinthian church precisely because he will not tolerate the charismatic element setting itself up against the institutional. André Lemaire has rightly noted that "Paul does not intend to create anarchical communities, but permanent ones, therefore organized. In that respect . . . it would be a mistake to consider the situation in the church of Corinth as an ideal, when Paul intervenes there with the definite purpose of restoring order."[4]

Inner Verification

The authentic person will find in his inner depths indications of the presence and operation of the Holy Spirit. Inclinations and decisions born of this Spirit bear traits that those born of selfishness or the world do not bear. Yet to speak of inner indications, inclinations and decisions is to speak of subjectivity, and to speak of subjectivity is to speak of the possibility of illusion. Hence not any inner experience is an inner verification that the Holy Spirit has spoken. We must study what this experience is and is not.

It is not always understood by those who are interested in discernment that the peace experience is of two types. On the one hand, there is the habitual inner harmony of the person following faithfully the lead of the indwelling Lord. On the other, there is the "ad hoc peace" that ac-

---

[4] André Lemaire, *Biblical Theology Bulletin*, June 1973, p. 156.

companies the decision prompted by the Spirit. The two
are related, but they should not be confused. The latter is
appreciated and of sign value in conjunction with the
former.

Habitual Inner Peace/Joy

Inner harmony, individual and communal, is a normal
state of affairs. Disorder and conflict are illnesses. The
virtuous person experiences "all joy" (Prov 10:28; Ps
64:11; 132:9), his light burns brightly (Prov 13:9; Ps
97:11), and he possesses a universal peace (Ps 119:165).
The man who looks to the Lord radiates a joy from his
inner encounter (Ps 34:5). When God is near, good
people sing for joy; they exult and rejoice (Ps 68:3-4, 32).
One must conclude that the normal human condition—
it *is* normal to be close to God—is to experience an abiding joy. In the days of the promised king, a universal
peace will abide without end (Ps 72:7), for he wills peace
for his friends if only they will renounce foolishness (Ps
85:8). They who learn to praise God enjoy his light and
continually exult in him (Ps 89:15–16; Ps 105:3): prayer-
fulness begets perception and peace. The person who
calls on God in his troubles finds an immediate response
in a divinely given comfort and happiness and joy in the
midst of all his troubles (2 Cor 7:4). A man of peace enjoys an abiding peace somehow received through the
Lord's representatives (Lk 10:5-6).

Ecclesial communities enjoy peace/joy as a sign of the
Holy Spirit's presence in their midst (Acts 9:31; 13:52;
CCC 1832). The Philippians are to rejoice always (not
only occasionally) and to experience a peace so marvelous
that it surpasses understanding (Phil 4:4, 7). The very

kingdom of Christ consists in goodness, joy and peace brought by the Spirit (Rom 14:17). Jesus had already promised that the Paraclete he would send to indwell would bring a peace the world cannot give, a complete joy, a joy no one can take away, a joy that is full (Jn 14:27; 15:11; 16:22, 33; 17:13). Peter tells his Christians that they do enjoy this kind of delight in God, a delight so remarkable it cannot be described in words (1 Pet 1:8). This harmony is to reign habitually in the hearts of the faithful (Col 3:15), always and in every way (2 Th 3:16).

These data of revelation aid us no little in dissipating common misunderstandings of what the peace experience of discernment is and is not. We may begin with the "is not". This inner harmony is not psychologically produced by human techniques, oriental or occidental. It is divinely given. Nor is it the mere cessation of conflict or the feeling of well-being at getting one's own way. It is not a sporadic thing, here today and gone tomorrow. Nor is it necessarily accompanied by a felt awareness of God's presence. A sensible awareness of the divine nearness is not a sure witness to his presence, just as dryness and desolation are not an indication of his absence. As a matter of fact, the purest, deepest knowledge of God is dark. Hence when we think we have a good, clear idea of him, we are probably farther away than when we meet him in the darkness of faith.

Now we may say positively what this habitual peace is. It is an inner harmony, an integrity born of goodness. Whole things flourish. A machine lacking oil or with a part missing is hardly "at peace". It squeaks or grinds or self-destructs or does not run at all. A human person who lacks love or honesty or purity or justice is necessarily a disordered human being. He cannot have inner peace because he is missing "parts". On the other hand, a person who is led by the Holy Spirit does possess the love and goodness poured out by him.

Our English concept of peace is fairly jejune. It refers chiefly in the popular mind to a cessation of hostility, a calm after battle. The ancient Hebrew concept included tranquility but much more besides. The root from which *shalom* comes signifies completion, finishing, perfection, fullness.[5] *Shalom*, the usual greeting, referred to a gift from the Lord God. It was a state of full well-being, a completeness that included of course a vibrant relationship with God. Peace, therefore, included holiness of life and in this sense prosperity. In the New Testament Jesus is the prince of peace, for in him the fullness of divine blessings is present. This peace, this fullness, the world cannot give. It is his gift and his alone (Jn 14:27). He is our peace and the announcer of the good news of it (Eph 2:14, 17).

When we examine even briefly the origins of our inner conflicts, we readily see why only the saintly person enjoys a full peace. Until we are purified, all of us are beset with a network of disorderly desires, or, as St. Paul would call them, illusory desires. And they who think they have the least most likely have the most. These illusions stem in turn from disorderly passions: avarice, lust, laziness, pride. To take the last as an illustration: in how many ways we suffer inner conflicts because of our vanities of a hundred types, our refusals to be corrected by others, our tenden-

---

[5] Speaking of *charis* (favor) and *eirene* (peace), Joseph A. Fitzmyer has noted that "the two words are Paul's summation of the *bona messianica* of the Christian era" (JBC 47:8). Raymond Brown has observed that "in Johannine language 'peace,' 'truth,' 'light,' 'life,' and 'joy,' are figurative terms reflecting different facets of the great gift that Jesus has brought from the Father to men" (*The Gospel according to John*, Anchor Bible, vols. 29–29A [Garden City, N.Y.: Doubleday, 1966–70], p. 653).

cies to dominate others, our unreasonable ambitions ("I must be first, the best . . ."), our self-centeredness (which others are constantly frustrating), our envy, our human respect. We suffer inner discord from our clashing pursuits. We try to serve God and mammon, and our resulting dead-end desires bear witness to the impossibility. Some of us learn the lesson, and some do not. Those who do learn are the spiritually mature, the virtuous. They are at peace.

This habitual harmony is not emotionally felt (although the feelings may or may not accompany it). It is delicate, quiet, spiritual.[6] It is not produced by human effort but is given by the Holy Spirit himself. A distinction mentioned by St. John of the Cross may be useful at this point. He differentiates active joy from passive. The first is humanly produced, can be controlled and is concerned with a clear object. The other is divinely produced, cannot be humanly intensified or prolonged, and it has no clear object. It seems to arise from no detectable cause.[7]

In chapter 3 we devoted considerable attention to an analysis of the experience of God. We found it both rich and diversified with many types, blends and intensities. Much the same is to be said of the habitual peace of which we speak in this chapter, for it is a facet of the experience of God. At one time it is a dark, purifying resting in God, at another it is joyous and loving. It can leave one with a sense of refreshment, a calm awareness of beauty, a tranquil joy in God. At another it may be a strong feeling of being engulfed in him, penetrated and embraced by him. This peace brings an experience of well-being, of silent power, strength, freedom.

---

[6] St. John of the Cross, *Dark Night*, bk. 1, chap. 9, no. 7; p. 315.
[7] See *Ascent*, bk. 3, chap. 17, no. 1; p. 239.

Because this infused peace derives from God, it is not related to a particular object or cause. A humanly caused peace can easily be traced to a specific cause: the resolution of a conflict, the avoidance of a catastrophic evil, the attainment of one's ambition, the reconciliation of friends, the solution of a problem. The peace given by the indwelling Spirit seems to well up from no cause. It is the result (indeed caused by God) of a person's being whole with a wholeness received from the divine self-communication.

Karl Rahner observes that this peace can bring a certitude of its divine origin. "Regarded purely in itself, it cannot deceive and in it God himself is present and nothing else at all can be. . . . Pure openness and receptivity is always genuine and can miss nothing because it excludes nothing but includes all."[8] We have shown in an earlier chapter that one may misinterpret this peace and draw invalid conclusions from it, but that does not make it illusory in itself.

The Matching Verification

Yet the general experience of infused peace is not of itself the inner confirmation we seek. More is needed. The New Testament speaks also of an actual peace as distinct from the habitual, that is, a peace that accompanies a particular proposal, decision, activity. St. Paul assures the Romans that what he is about to say to them is the truth, and he knows it because he speaks in union with Christ, and his conscience in union with the Holy Spirit assures him of it (Rom 9:1). Later in the same letter, the apostle teaches that the kingdom of God does not consist in eating

[8] *The Dynamic Element in the Church* (New York: Herder and Herder, 1964), p. 149.

or drinking this or that but in goodness and peace and joy brought by the Holy Spirit (Rom 14:17). He concludes that we ought consequently to adopt practices that lead to peace (Rom 14:19). In other words, people who habitually enjoy life in the new creation and possess goodness/peace/joy find that wise choices bring further peace. Action fits habit. A decision emanating from the Holy Spirit does not disturb or jar the abiding calm also given by the same Spirit.

This is true not only in the individual person but also in a community. A group that habitually enjoys the harmony given by the Spirit (Gal 5:22) finds that both its communal decisions and the actions of the members fit into the normal calm. In his teaching on the regulation of charismatic gifts in the community, St. Paul lays it down that genuine prophets can control their gifts because "God is not a God of disorder but of peace" (1 Cor 14:32–33). We find the same teaching in the Letter of James. Genuine wisdom from above brings peace, whereas wickedness brings disharmony (James 3:16–17).

The peace-matching of concrete action and habitual peace needs illustration so that we may see how the matching verifies the divine origin of the action (inclination, decision). A scholar skilled in the style and content of an ancient writer (for example, Caesarius of Arles) knows thoroughly the ideas, vocabulary, mannerisms, grammatical peculiarities, source dependencies and temperamental characteristics of his author. He has imbibed the very spirit of his writings. If some new manuscript should be unearthed, this scholar could tell without much difficulty whether its author was Caesarius or not. The new case matches or does not match the known habitual material. So also the person skilled in the "style and content" of the

Holy Spirit can, as it were, match this new inclination, idea, proposal against the Spirit's usual gift. If the former jars the latter, it is not from the Spirit. If it fits like the last piece in a jigsaw puzzle, it is from him.

I was once visiting a religious formation center and was given a formation manual to examine. As I paged through the book, I suddenly came across a page whose contents, style and mode of expression were immediately familiar to me. The reason? The page had been incorporated without quotation marks from something I had published earlier. Once again the "new case" matched perfectly with the old.

The inner verification, therefore, is a religious experience.[9] It is not a contentment consequent on finding an agreeable solution. It can happen only in one who lives in a habitual union with God, one who knows what contemplative communion is about and at least to some extent lives in that communion. This observation should be extended, it seems to me, also to communal discernment. A group of worldly minded people may discuss and even pray together and yet be quite devoid of the habitual peace born of deepening prayer. They consequently lack the habitual gift with which to match their specific proposals. The "peace" they may feel at the end of their deliberations is not the inner verification of which we are speaking.

[9] This seems to be the "consolation", the "*sentir*" of St. Ignatius of Loyola in his practice of discernment. "This felt consolation", says a recent writer, "which accompanies the consideration of a possible course of action becomes for Ignatius the norm of action. . . . In this way Ignatius used consolation as a clue to reach practical decisions in his apostolate, not casually or sporadically, but systematically. He was always the pilgrim, always searching for God's will, always confident of finding it, and therefore he monitored his consciousness day by day for evidence of consolation" (William J. Walsh, S.J., reviewing deVries' work on discernment in *Theological Studies*, December 1973, p. 728).

This peace/joy sign is fallible, of course, and that is why we need external verification also. But the fallibility ought not to be exaggerated. Orsy seemed so to exaggerate it in his view that peace and joy are indicators of a person's or community's relation to God and not necessarily that a decision is objectively the best or the wisest.[10] There are several questionable assumptions in this position. One is that the discerning process is to yield the "best and the wisest among options". I would not hold this. God takes our limitations into account and can give his peace as a sign that we have chosen a suitable, even if not the best, option. Historical examples apparently to the contrary are appropriate only if one interprets them correctly. To cite the rejection by St. Francis of Assisi's disciples of the saint's discernment as an indication that Francis' peace was not a sign of his detecting God's will is to miss a much more obvious explanation of the rejection, namely, that those rejecting had not discerned what God wanted of them as Francis had. More than once St. Paul makes the point that when the community at Corinth or in Galatia is divided, there is sin and immaturity in at least some of the members. Then, too, peace/joy must be a sign in usual circumstances, for a sign that is a sign only half of the time is hardly a sign at all.

Outer Verification

Our earlier section on obedience as a sign of the Spirit provides ample biblical evidence implying the need for private persons to be tested by the hierarchical element in the Church. These we will not repeat. More to our point

[10] Ladislas Orsy, S.J., "Toward a Theological Evaluation of Communal Discernment", *Studies in the Spirituality of Jesuits*, October 1973, pp. 180–81.

will be the exploration of those New Testament data that make explicit the need in the *ekklesia* for the structural offices to assess and approve private initiatives that affect the life of the community in important ways.

Already in the chronologically first of the New Testament writings we find St. Paul expressing awareness that the Holy Spirit himself stands behind the apostle's teaching. Anyone who objects to Paul's instruction is objecting "not to a human authority but to God" (1 Th 4:8). The private idea cedes to the official decision. This same thought is presented in vigorous language and imagery in the first chapter of Galatians. Even if an angel from heaven (a private "source") were to reveal to the Galatians something other than what they had heard from the human lips of their leaders, he is to be anathema (Gal 1:6-9). A supposed messenger from heaven itself must be tested by human representatives of the Lord, not the other way around.

What Paul taught he practiced. He who received an undoubted revelation from the risen Lord is instructed by God to go to Jerusalem and seek the approval of the "leading men" (Gal 2:2). This he obediently does. The official structure tests and approves the individual commission, not the other way around.

But, one may ask, what of the free "charismatics" in Corinth? Who tested them? The answer to this question is simple: Paul did. Unwary enthusiasts enjoy pointing to Corinth as a biblical antecedent for their view of an unstructured Church. Careful scholars avoid this mistake. They note that precisely because some of the Corinthians disregarded authority figures, their church in Paul's mind was quite the opposite of a model *ekklesia*. He roundly condemned their free-wheeling approach and their factions—this is the first item of business he took up in his First Letter. While there is no mention of a local testing authority (yet silence does not prove there was none), St. Paul himself leaves no doubt that the private views and charisms of the Corinthians are subject to his authority. Even the "free" Corinthian community must accept the outer structural verification of their gifts. Competent biblical scholarship quite thoroughly rejects the fairly widespread notion today that private persons are to test hierarchical activity and not vice versa. In a recent example we read apropos of St. Paul giving the Corinthians strict rules for the regulation of authentic charisms:

> This intrusion of the apostle into a domain in which the activity of the Spirit manifests itself shows that in all cases the charisms remain subjected to ecclesiastical authority. As long as the apostles are living, their power in this matter comes from the fact that the apostolate is the primary charism. After them their delegates participate also in the same authority as the instructions gathered from the pastoral epistles show (especially 1 Tim 1:18–4:16). This is because these delegates themselves have received a particular gift of the Spirit by the imposition of hands (1 Tim 4:14; 2 Tim 1:6). If they are not able to possess the charism of the apostles, nevertheless they have no less a charism of government which gives them the right to prescribe and to teach (1 Tim 4:11) and which no one ought to look down on (1 Tim 4:12). In the Church everything remains subjected to the hierarchy of government which is itself of charismatic order.[11]

---

[11] Augustin George and Pierre Grelot, in DBT 57. The pastorals are so insistent on doctrinal purity that Gerard Therrien, in *Le Discernement dans les écrits pauliniens* (Paris: J. Gabalda, 1973), can say of the four discernment passages (1 Tim 3:10; 2 Tim 2:15; 3:8; Titus 1:16): "Nos quatre textes se rapportent—directement ou en creux—à l'homme apostolique dans sa responsabilité de transmettre la saine doctrine et de défendre la communauté contre les faux docteurs" (p. 218). "Il s'agit [in Tim 2:15] avant

St. Paul goes so far as to say that if anyone in Corinth claims to be inspired by God and does not acknowledge Paul's teaching as divinely authorized, that person is shown by his very action not to be an authentic prophet. The rest in the community ought not to follow him (1 Cor 14:37–38).[12]

St. Paul is not alone in subordinating the individual prophetic person to the external structural elements in the ecclesial community. We read, for example, that "Luke portrays the earliest church as greatly influenced by 'pneumatic,' prophetic men, guided by prophetic experiences at the crucial moments of its history (e.g., 10:1–48; 13:1–3; 15:1–32). Yet he tends to relegate prophets to the fringes of those scenes in which church leaders are engaged in policy-making decisions."[13] This same position is operative in the Johannine communities. Toward the end of the first century, private teachers who contradicted the

---

tout d'un charisme d'assurance et d'orthodoxie dans la prédication." This, he says, is "la préoccupation fondamentale des Pastorales" (p. 221).

[12] On this text, cf. John J. O'Rourke, in *A New Catholic Commentary on Holy Scripture* (Nashville: Nelson, 1975), p. 1158. Another Scripture scholar comments on this crucial text: "Paul has now surely said the last word on this point. One feels in his sentences how great was the inclination of the Corinthians to judge everything from their own point of view and to question everything again and again. Against this Paul established decisively that no one is a Christian for himself alone, so that he has only to judge according to his own insight. Being a Christian is only possible as a member of Christ's body and therefore by integration and subordination. It may be that 'in itself' there is always something more that could be said against it, but this cannot come from a good spirit. . . . The man who is not willing to recognize it is not recognized by God" (Eugen Walter, *The First Epistle to the Corinthians*, NTSR 13 (New York: Herder and Herder, 1971), pp. 154–55.

[13] M. Eugene Boring, "How May We Identify Oracles of Christian Prophets in the Synoptic Tradition? Mark 3:28–29 as a Test Case", *Journal of Biblical Literature*, December 1972, p. 502.

official teaching of the leaders are judged by the latter and are known to lack the "spirit of truth" precisely because they reject the leaders' teaching. Once again the private charismatic is judged by the structural element, not vice versa (1 Jn 4:1-6). Ecumenical studies are now accepting more and more of the Petrine office in the first-century Church. In a recent joint work we read regarding 2 Peter 3:15–16:

> Obviously, in II Peter the shepherdship of Peter is being applied in a different way from that encountered in I Peter; and the primary emphasis is now on Peter as the guardian of orthodox faith—a possible facet of the presbyter-shepherd, as we saw in Acts 20:28–30. His apostolic authority enables him to judge interpretations of Scripture, even the writings of another apostle. We can now speak of a "Petrine magisterium," perhaps related to an application of the binding/loosing power we saw in Matthew.[14]

The confirming function of external authority begun in the apostolic age was continued by the transferral to successors of an ecclesial power to govern and teach. As the first century wears on, we find a number of references to the imposing of hands as the means of conferring spiritual authority: Acts 6:6; 13:13; 1 Timothy 4:14; 5:22. Regarding these passages, a Scripture commentator notes, "The symbolism is the communication of power and authority. And the solidarity of those who impose hands and those who receive the imposition is affirmed. The imposition of hands which Timothy received conferred upon him a grace. By the time 1 Tim was written the imposition of

---

[14] *Peter in the New Testament*, ed. Raymond E. Brown, Karl P. Donfried and John Reumann (Minneapolis: Augsburg Pub. House, 1973), pp. 155–56. The same point is made again pp. 166–67.

hands seems to have become the normal rite of ordination to office in the Church." [15]

Why an Outer Verification?

The activities of the Holy Spirit occur within a community, the *qahal*, assembly of the Lord, the Temple Church. God does not reveal himself to private individuals operating at cross-purposes and in mutual contradiction. He is a God who makes sense. This is why we speak in theology of the analogy of faith. Speaking of diverse gifts in the Church, St. Paul tells the Romans that he with the gift of prophecy is to use it "according to his faith" or "in proportion to his faith" (Rom 12:6). This means that a person proclaiming the message should understand and explain it in harmony with the totality of revelation and the official teaching of the Church. They who test the "spirits" use the analogy of faith as one of the touchstones of authenticity. In both Testaments the man or woman who departs from known revelation, from the faith of the community, is immediately known as not coming from God. Outer verification is a protection of the community from those who would disrupt its inner coherence. One does not accept Christ piecemeal.

The necessity of an outer testing structure in the Church arises also from the very nature of human society. A common and often unrealized presupposition of anti-authority positions is the insufficiency theory of human governing. In this view, authority is necessary in mental institutions, in prisons and among children. Some people are unable or unwilling to direct themselves. Hence,

[15] McKenzie, *Dictionary*, p. 385.

when a society matures, its members slowly lose the need for directions from superiors. It is not accidental that people who now commonly speak of our generation as "men come of age" are often those who belittle the need for societal government.

The truth in this position is that, as Yves Simon so well showed in his works on authority, substitutional authority (exercised in behalf of children, prisoners, patients) is one type of authority and reflects one type of need. The error in this position lies in its partiality. It fails to provide for the many other needs among perfectly adult men and women that cannot be met by what Simon calls the essential role of authority. No matter how mature a society has become, its members cannot provide for protection, for international trade, for airports and highways (and a host of other things) by mere friendly agreements. To desire to substitute consensus as a universal replacement for authority is merely utopian. When the members of a group are all open to the Holy Spirit, a discernment process can produce consensus, but who will maintain that in our sinful condition we can hope in larger societies to be free from selfishness and ignorances of all sorts. And even aside from our sinfulness, we need to note that "all judgments made for an action are surrounded with contingencies that make it impossible to demonstrate the necessity of any given prudential judgment." [16] One of the functions of authority, therefore, is to choose among many defensible courses of action one that all must follow.

When a group opts to have no official leadership, it does not follow that it shall have no leadership. It shall. And it may be more demanding (sometimes tyrannical) than an

[16] G. J. McMorrow, "Authority", NCE 1:1112.

appointed or elected leadership. When the latter is tyrannical, there is usually an appeal to a higher authority or to another election. When leaders unofficially emerge, there is sometimes no appeal at all. There are struggles, power struggles, silent suffering.

This sort of phenomenon occurs also in matters theological. If a group of people rejects an official teaching authority in the Church, it does not follow that there is no teaching authority. There surely is, and often it is more apodictic and harsh in its condemnations than most popes have ever been. The allegiance given to quotations from "in" theologians can be remarkable. It has been noted that in Protestantism university theologians have an influence "analogous to that of the hierarchical magisterium in the Catholic Church".[17]

The binding force of an ecclesiastical Magisterium is commonly viewed as an infringement on a healthy freedom in the academic realm. It is no more an infringement on freedom than the experimental data of the positive sciences are an impediment to scientific progress and freedom. The divinely guaranteed Magisterium liberates the theologian from the morass of his own subjectivity just as the hard-nosed data of scientific research liberate the theoretician in pure physics from the illusions of a thought lacking contact with the real world. If one thinks I am here romanticizing the Church's teaching authority, I invite him to look into past and current theological history. It is alleged that Roman congregations have made mistakes and that these impede progress. Some (not all) of these allegations are true. But in sheer number they are few indeed in comparison to the thousands of mistakes that

---

[17] M. B. Schepers, NCE 11:886.

theologians have made. And I mean mistakes that are commonly admitted to have been mistakes, even blunders. Luther and Calvin made more errors in theology than one would care to number. A contemporary theologian in one decade will sometimes abandon totally a position he held ten years previously. An outer-verification principle indeed liberates the faithful in their pursuance of truth. History abounds in examples of the bizarre aberrations possible even in well-intentioned enthusiasms. "'The task of giving an authentic interpretation of the Word of God, whether in its written form or the form of Tradition, has been entrusted to the living, teaching office of the Church alone. Its authority in this matter is exercised in the name of Jesus Christ' (DV 10.2). This means that the task of interpretation has been entrusted to the bishops in communion with the successor of Peter, the Bishop of Rome" (CCC 85). The structural elements in the Church provide us bodily beings with a handy means to distinguish the Holy Spirit from an unholy spirit.

12

KEY TO GOSPEL MORALITY

According to his upbringing, the common man usually looks upon morality in one of two ways. Either it is a code of precepts and prohibitions, or it is a vague, subjective feeling of what seems right. In the first view, morality is learned in the home and in the church. It is something given, clear, objective, covering most, if not all, cases. In the second view, morality is not properly learned at all. It is something one experiences in a given situation. It is not clear, not objective, and it covers only one case at a time. Each man is his own judge.

The professional ethicist is usually more sophisticated, but he is not always completely free from our two simplistic views. One need only examine the abundance of current ethical writing to see that too many moralists write as though intellectual analysis were the chief tool in discovering gospel morality. Much, if not most, of their time is spent in their own reasonings and in evaluating one another's theories. Some hold that morality is objective, something to be learned, while others subscribe to the subjective decision freed from absolute norms.

More perceptive thinkers know that both of these trends are myopic and largely alien to New Testament thinking about knowing the moral good. St. Paul, for example, does not spend a great deal of time reasoning to moral conclusions, and he surely does not hold that morality is a subjective feeling of propriety that each person determines for himself. For the apostle, there is an objective moral code, yes, and there are universal prohibitions. These are taught by the Church (Paul continually propounds binding moral teaching), and they must be followed.[1] Saying this, however, does not touch the heart of his concept of knowing the morality of the new creation.

For Paul, the indwelling Spirit is the supreme moral norm (Rom 8:2), and that man knows moral goodness and badness who is finely attuned to this Spirit. In other words, only the holy person knows morality in an adequate manner. When the apostle writes of knowing the perfect will of God (and not, therefore, of a mere minimal, is-it-a-sin? morality), he speaks not in terms of a code, but of a sheer goodness that can detect the mind of the Lord himself. He admonishes the Romans not to model their lives on the behavior of the world about them but rather to undergo a conversion. This, says he, "is the only way to discover God's will, to know what is good, what God wants, what is the perfect course of action" (Rom 12:2 JB). Subjective feeling is not enough. Abstract reasoning is not enough. Scholarly criticism is not enough. Conversion of morals and sanctity of life are demanded.

It goes without saying that the saintly person listens to the moral teaching of the Church. That itself is one of the signs of his authentic sanctity: "He who hears you, hears

---

[1] The divisions in the Corinthian church seem to have been in ethical interpretations rather than in the kerygma they had received. See Raymond E. Brown, Karl P. Donfried and John Reumann, *Peter in the New Testament* (Minneapolis: Augsburg Pub. House, 1973), p. 36.

me." But nonetheless there are a thousand moral applications of moral teaching that each person must discover and live for himself. The moral good is best known through connaturality, for he who loves knows God (1 Jn 4:7–8), and God is the epitome of goodness. For St. Paul, one does not become adept in knowing right and wrong merely by patient and prolonged study of principles. Useful as this is, it is by no means enough. One becomes adept in moral knowledge in proportion to his advance in holiness. Paul's prayer for the Philippians is that through a growing love their perception may deepen, and thus they may always recognize what is best (Phil 1:9).

The Holy Spirit leads his own into the knowledge of the complete truth (Jn 16:13; cf. also 14:26). God has a unique design on each person even though all of us are to be immersed into the one deification flowing from the enthralling vision of Father, Son and Spirit. This unique design is not accomplished solely by our fulfillment of universal precepts. These universal precepts form us, but the individualized leading of the Spirit is also needed, for they are sons of God who are led by the Spirit of God (Rom 8:14).

We have here a revolution in the field of ethics. Yet it receives scant attention from the professional moralists even though Oscar Cullman has called our attention to the fact that discernment is the key to New Testament morality.

Through the sending of the Holy Spirit into our hearts, Jesus has given us a new principle of morality and the knowledge of good and evil. He has removed our stony hearts and given us warm, loving hearts capable of grasping the mind of God. Since divine thoughts and ways are not human thoughts and ways, we can expect that gospel morality is going to surpass by far our human tendency to minimalism and the easy road.

The Spirit dwelling within the Church brings to her mind all that Jesus has taught (Jn 14:26) so that they who articulate the teachings of Jesus to the community actually speak in his name: "He who hears you, hears me." This is why for New Testament writers the normal way to learn moral principles is to listen to the leaders of the *ekklesia*, just as it was the normal way in the old dispensation.

Yet the principles have to be applied to the concrete situations of daily life. Here, too, the indwelling Spirit is operative. Just as he teaches through his guidance of pope and bishops, so he guides the holy man and woman in applying that teaching to their daily lives. Obviously the second type of guidance does not contradict the first. It is universally characteristic of the saints that they wholeheartedly embrace the doctrinal and moral teaching of their pastors. Because of their love, humility and obedience, they are therefore capable of perceiving the inner movings of the Spirit in their hearts and thus of applying ecclesial teachings rightly.

Scripture knows nothing of God moving people to set aside the moral teaching of his representatives. What God does do is further enlighten his faithful ones to know perfectly how to apply this teaching to concrete cases, how to live the sufferings implied in the paschal mystery, how to draw good from evil, how to make the sacrifices inherent in living gospel morality, how to rejoice in the Lord always.

Because the Holy Spirit is the first gospel law, one knows moral goodness to the extent that he is receptive to the inner enlightenments of the Spirit within. That is why the man or woman of deep prayer can detect moral evil where the mere technician may see only a pragmatic utility. That is why the holy person does not succumb to the pressures of what the world is ready to accept or live. He does not suffer the blunting and suffocating and dulling effects of "the concerns and riches and pleasures of life" (Lk 8:14). The eye of his mind is clear, fresh, perceptive. Whereas the worldly man cannot understand the things of the Spirit (1 Cor 2:14), the converted person does understand.

This doctrine is not an anti-intellectualism. It implies neither a disregard for academic ethics nor a neglect of sound moral teaching in classroom and pulpit. But it does imply a personal holiness both in the moralist and in the learner. Without that holiness, the divine mind is simply not accessible. Academics can attain human wisdom, perhaps much of it. But academics by themselves do not attain divine wisdom. Hans Urs von Balthasar has rightly pointed out that the saints are "the great history of the interpretation of the gospel, more genuine and with more power of conviction than all exegesis. They are the proof both of the fullness and of the presence."[2]

It is in this sense (as well as in others) that the saints are the best advertisement for the Church's life and teaching. They have an evangelical-ecclesial sense that the lesser of us have either only in a diminished degree or in no degree at all. The saint knows by an instinct of the Holy Spirit who is the true prophet genuinely proclaiming the mind of the Lord and who is the false prophet proclaiming his own mind. The saint easily detects sound morality according to the purity of Christ Jesus and perhaps even more easily detects the worldly rationalizations that seek to justify selfish morality.

---

[2] *Elucidations* (London: SPCK, 1975), p. 81.

The biblical idea that men fail to reach the light because their will is not free from sin has been said in another classical way (attributed to Caesar): "*Homines semper quod volunt credunt*—that which men will they always believe." The current controversy over contraception is a case in point. No persuasive intellectual case for artificial contraception has been presented by anyone, and yet significant segments of the human family profess a belief that it is licit. The same is true of recent attempts to justify masturbation, premarital sexuality, homosexuality, adultery and abortion. A cardinal but rarely admitted premise to all the argumentation is that sexual pleasure must be allowed to consenting persons for its own sake. Moral principles must be wrong if they impede or prevent sexual pleasure as frequently as one may wish it. Not even a likely abortion may stand in the way of what men and women (or boys and girls) want. "That which men will they always believe."

This is not the place to review the recent literature supporting the sound sexual morality of the gospel and the Church's long teaching, but it is intriguing to imagine what the current situation would be like if sexual activity were not pleasurable. There would be no attempt at all to justify rejection of the Church's teaching. No one would have questioned it. Positively blocking the procreative function of sexual activity would be viewed as a perversion of its obvious purpose. If someone had proposed the current arguments for masturbation, contraception and the rest, they would have been seen immediately as specious.

The pleasure principle is powerful not only in the bodies of men and women but also in their minds and wills. Sense pleasures are good, not bad. But they are not the final purpose of human life nor its chief value. They are supportive, ancillary to far greater things. Sense pleasures sought for themselves to the neglect of what they accompany (a contradiction to Paul's "whether you eat or drink or do anything else, do all for the glory of God"—1 Cor 10:31) are an upsetting of the divine economy. The more they are sought in and for themselves, the more the person weakens his commitment to selfless devotion to others, to serious study, most of all to a deep immersion in prayerful communion with God. Jesus himself put his finger on this truth when he explained that the word of God does not mature in those who are smothered by the cares, the riches and the pleasures of life (Lk 8:14).

This is true both of individuals and of society. A community that centers its life on pleasure-seeking becomes pragmatic rather than principled. Its commitments to honesty in speech, to justice in work and wages and to sacrifice for the good of others are all slowly debilitated. It is not accidental that permissive sexual morality is accompanied by a rising crime rate.

The signs of the Holy Spirit that we have already discussed point to the authentic teacher of moral theology: humility, love, sound doctrine, obedience to superiors and carrying of the cross, at odds with the spirit of the world. These same signs indicate who is applying the principles of gospel morality correctly to his concrete situations. We see this truth age after age in the simple, unpretentious lives of the faithful laity. With no need to court popularity, they quietly live the purity of the Church's moral teaching, and they readily listen to the inner enlightenments of the Holy Spirit. They would be the last to claim a privileged pipeline to the mind of God, but they are the very ones who are taught the mysteries of the Father (Lk 10:21). Simple men and women of prayer are far more reliable guides to gospel morality than are those who, filled with a sense of their own wisdom, endlessly cite one another in their footnotes and pay scant serious attention (that is, obediential attention) to the teaching of the Magisterium.

Gospel Morality: A Revolution

From the fact that the Holy Spirit is the first gospel moral law, it follows that a gospel morality will be more than slightly different from a naturalist ethical system. Isaiah has told us that God's thoughts are not our thoughts and his ways are not our ways. If one is not listening to the Holy Spirit, it is not surprising that his moral views are indistinguishable from the non-Christian ethician. But if he is listening to the Spirit speaking in the Church (Rev 2:7), he will proclaim a morality that the spirit of the world is by no means disposed to accept.

New Testament morality is not a restatement of Aristotelian or Platonic or Kantian ethics; nor is it a collection of universal, abstract principles that alone suffice to settle concrete ethical questions by their mere application. The principal law of the new creation is the indwelling Spirit, who leads from within. He calls the individual as an individual, and though he will not contradict either gospel principles or the Church's teaching, he does uniquely call unique persons. Perceptivity, a capacity to detect this call, lies, therefore, at the heart of the Christic enterprise.

We can no more deduce the divine plan for us by an intensive scrutiny of our own nature and/or circumstances, by a careful looking within or without, than a duck could imagine Mozart or Shakespeare by turning its attention (if it could) to its own duckiness. Eye has not seen nor ear heard what God has in store.

Our unaided reasoning is pitifully inadequate to moral judgment as leading to our genuine fulfillment. Unaided reason cannot suspect the enthrallment for which we are made. Reason is content with the dull least. Doctor Johnson has said, "If a bull could speak, he might as well exclaim, 'Here I am with this cow and this grass; what being can enjoy better felicity?'" The current tyranny of normless morality and the despair to which it leads (a recent book bears the title *Marriage Is Hell*) is sufficient suggestion.

There are several reasons why Christian morality differs from a natural or pagan morality not only in orientation and motivation but also in content:

1. *The Gospel presents a sublime content of holiness that non-Christian codes do not attain.* We are to love our enemies, do good to those who hate and persecute us, to rejoice in our sufferings, to share material goods with our brother to the point of equality with him, to pray always and everywhere, to subordinate work to prayer, to carry a cross every day. Only at the price of minimalism that omits whole areas of gospel activity could one maintain that the content of Christian ethics is not significantly different from any other.

2. *The Christian's main concern is communion with the Father, Son and Spirit.* Johannine morality especially brings this out, and it is light years from a pagan morality.[3] If one

---

[3] See André Feuillet, P.S.S., "La Morale chrétienne d'après Saint Jean", *Esprit et Vie*, November 15, 1973, p. 666. Feuillet cites J. Bonsirven: Johannine morality, he says, "est foncièrement mystique. À l'encontre d'un moralisme naturel ou d'un ascétisme étroit, elle ne s'attache pas, uniquement ou principalement, à édicter des consignes pratiques, destinées à

objects that this makes moral theology a part of spiritual theology, I can only answer: Of course. The cleavage between these two is most unfortunate. It suggests that moral theology is a minimalistic science of human activity meant for the masses, whereas "spiritual theology" is maximalistic and meant for an elite. The gospel makes no such distinction. Nor should we.

3. *Christian morality is primarily vertical, secondarily horizontal.* The primary concern is doing all for the glory of the Father (1 Cor 10:31), singing to him in our hearts always and everywhere (Eph 5:19–20), loving him with a whole heart, soul and mind (Lk 10:27). A natural morality is either predominantly or even exclusively a horizontal matter, a relating with one's fellow men. This is a vast difference in content as well as in motivation.

4. *For us, action for the brother is subordinated to contemplation of the Father* (SC no. 2). For a secular ethics, action is all there is. Again the difference is vast. One can fail to see it only if he fails to accept in a meaningful way the whole gospel message.

5. *Gospel morality is shot through with the sign of the cross.* We live only if we are cast into the earth like the seed and die (Jn 12:24). We who are baptized are crucified with Christ that we may rise with him (Rom 6:3–6). We take suffering for the kingdom to be our normal lot (1 Pet 4:12–13). We are so different in our actions that we expect to be persecuted as a sure consequence of living the new

---

promouvoir une excellence et une perfection tout humaines; elle recherche avant tout la communion avec Dieu, la participation à certaines propriétés divines: verité, lumière, amour, parole de Dieu; celui qui demeure en ces principes feconds et en qui ces principes demeurent est assuré de parvenir au sommet de la sainteté, de la ressemblance à Dieu" (p. 670).

message (Mt 5:10–12; 2 Tim 3:12). We are to carry a cross every day and renounce all that we possess (Lk 9:23; 14:33). We are to lose our old selves and be recreated in a moral revolution (Mt 16:25; Eph 4:22–24). In a naturalistic ethics we hear nothing of all this. The content is again vastly different.

6. *Gospel morality must include concern with the inner direction of the Holy Spirit and therefore the whole area of discernment.* They are sons of God who are led by the Spirit of God (Rom 8:14). While a secular ethics may be content with its reasoned norms, a revealed ethics cannot be so content. Our moral theology must be a discernment theology.

13

DISCERNMENT AND THEOLOGICAL PLURALISM

Built into the basic units of human society is a continuing tension between unity and diversity. Whether the unit be the family or city or state or church, there is an inner pull between the development of the unique person as unique and the cohesion and harmony of the social group as a group. Ideally there is no clash between a healthy pluralism and a strong unity. Each should promote the other. Practically it is a rare decade in history that sees a happy balance in most sectors of human life. More often one extreme or the other holds sway. Either diversity tends to be smothered under a rigid conformism, or unity is weakened by individualistic fragmentation.

But care must be taken here. We are not speaking of any diversity. The widespread divisions in the Church are not merely liberal–conservative differences, a politicization of the religious sphere. The cleavages run even more deeply into the levels of doctrine and principle. Theological differences of earlier ages were not called factions, because the various schools shared a common faith vision. This is not always true today. It would be difficult to mention many doctrines on which all theologians would unambiguously agree.

In the history of the Church, doctrinal differences do not long remain merely in the abstract order. Especially is this true in an age of mass media and instantaneous communication. These cleavages tend to crystallize into fixed positions regarding morality, liturgy, discipline, states of life. Soon the crystallized positions tend to beget indifference, in which the two groups agree to ignore each other, mutually to shun meetings, statements and literature issuing from the other side.

The unity-in-diversity problem in the Church today lies at the very heart of the Church's mission in the world. It is a problem that underlies worship, apostolate, ecumenism, theological progress, religious life. The secretary of the International Theological Commission speaks of relativism as "the new form of the eternal temptation of skepticism. . . . The attempt is no longer made to reach the facts but to describe personal reactions. . . . It is no longer a question of seeking or even esteeming the unity of truth but of recognizing and justifying differences of opinion among people." This scepticism, he notes, "is connected with an eternal heaviness, a resistance that man always puts up against divine truth".[1]

This scepticism is an intellectual illness. Just as our stomach is meant to receive, retain and use food for the benefit of the whole person, so is the intellect meant to receive, retain and use contact with the real and with its Author. A mind that cannot firmly embrace solid food is an ill mind.

One may object at this point that most cleavages among

[1] Philippe Delhaye, "Reflection on the Problem of Pluralism in the Church", *L'Osservatore Romano*, February 27, 1975, p. 7.

the faithful lie in the area of ethics and that the problem is not so much division in faith as it is a pluralism in practice. This observation may appear to take the edge off the fragmentation problem, but in reality it merely offers another example of how pervasive the faith problem is. One may not rightly maintain that opposing positions in moral theology have little to do with questions of faith for the reason that moral matters are not doctrinal matters. The right of the Magisterium to teach with a binding authority in the area of morals is itself a doctrinal matter. Serious Catholics are correct in feeling a clash between contraceptive practice, on the one hand, and their faith commitment, on the other. Jesus did not reveal an abstract pattern of doctrinal truth but rather a pattern of life itself inextricably interwoven with trinitarian, incarnational, ecclesial and eschatological implications. We just cannot divorce doctrinal theology from moral theology. And we may separate neither of them from spiritual theology. Thus people with problems about accepting the Magisterium's teaching in ethical matters should be aware of problems in faith and prayer.

Complementary Pluralism

It is remarkable how many theologians and religious journalists speak of pluralism in the Church as though it were quite undifferentiated. The same has been true of many religious superiors who have cheerily reacted to deep cleavages in their institutes by speaking of "unity in diversity", as though there were only one type of diversity. Reality has a way of avenging itself on those who slight it, and thus it has become increasingly clear that while some types of diversity are enriching, other types are destructive.

More perceptive thinkers nuance their statements. They note that a complementary pluralism is enriching to the community. In a joint statement, Lutheran and Catholic theologians remarked that all the members of the church "should recognize that the Spirit's guidance may give rise to diverse forms in piety, liturgy, theology, custom or law. Yet a variety of ecclesial types should never foster divisiveness."[2]

Joseph Ratzinger has written of the pluralistic interplay of Magisterium, theology and the faithful's lived experience of the gospel as all contributing to the Church's presentation of Christ to the world. All of us, simple and learned alike, live the reality of the Christ event. Theologians question and analyze. The Magisterium listens and decides. No one or two of these may operate independently in a rugged individualism.[3]

Ecclesiology furnishes us with apt illustrations of the richness found in complementary pluralism. We now speak routinely of the many biblical models of the Church, and we find that each of them throws a lightsome shaft of beauty on the reality of the *ekklesia*. There is the *people of God* model, which brings out the communal nature of the Church, her divine selection, her being called out of the darkness into the light of the Lord God. There is the *sacrament of Christ* model, which underlines the Church as the continuation of Jesus' presence in the world and the incarnational manner in which he applies his saving grace. There is the *pilgrim* model, which brings

[2] "Ministry and the Church Universal", statement of thirteen Lutheran and thirteen Catholic theologians on papal primacy, published in *Ecumenical Trends*, no. 1 (April 1974), p. 2.

[3] Joseph Ratzinger, "Magisterium of the Church, Faith, Morality", *L'Osservatore Romano*, December 26, 1974, p. 15.

out the on-the-wayness of the Church, the fact that we have here no lasting city, that, being co-pilgrims, we promote a sparing-sharing life-style and are concerned with our needy brothers and sisters as we journey with them. There is the Church as *event* model, which explains her as actualizing the work of Christ in her manifold activities, particularly in her proclamation of the word and the celebration of the Eucharist. There is the *hierarchical* model, which underlines the visible unity of God's people under Peter and his brothers and explains how through these offices we are preserved in the truth. There is the *Mystical Body* or *vine and branches* model, a model that makes obvious our close interdependence on one another and especially on the grace of Christ. There is the *temple* or *house of prayer* model, which brings out forcefully the purpose of all the other models, namely, that all of us share the call to a deep prayer life, a contemplation that will achieve its fullness when we shall see God as he is. These and other models of the Church are diversity at its best.[4] There is here nothing divisive, nothing contradictory, nothing destructive.

Pope Paul VI explicitly adverted to this pluralism question more than once in his statements. In one discourse he spoke at length of true and false pluralism, and he used an apt image to illustrate the healthy diversity of which we are speaking here: "We could compare the doctrinal pluralism of the Catholic Church to that of an orchestra", he

---

[4] Some other biblical images of the Church are virgin-bride of Christ, flock with a single shepherd, treasure in the field, wedding banquet. Avery Dulles' *Models of the Church* (Garden City, N.Y.: Doubleday, 1974) presents a schematic picture of several models. The book is clearly written, but it labors under limitations pointed out in critical reviews. On the one hand, it plays down excessively the institutional model, and, on the other, it exaggerates as a criterion of value what modern men find to their liking.

said, "in which the plurality of the instruments and the diversity of their respective parts combine to produce a single and admirable harmony."[5] The Holy Father later remarked that "harmony in the same faith is never immune from personal characteristics in the assent of each individual" but he points out that the essential content of the faith is not harmed because the diverse emphases "are unified in the common assent to the Church's magisterium".[6]

The enriching beauty of the many gifts and offices in the Church was taught by St. Paul himself (1 Cor 12:4–11; Eph 4:11–13). And yet in both contexts the apostle insists that this diversity is brought into a unity by the same Holy Spirit who dwells in all and binds all together in love and faith (1 Cor 12:12–13; Eph 4:1–6, 13).

Contradictory Pluralism

By contradictory pluralism I mean that direct opposition by which what is affirmed by one party is denied in the same sense by another. This diversity does not fill out, enrich, complement. Complementary statements may both be correct, while contradictory ones necessarily imply one error. One speaker must be out of touch with reality. The house cannot be green and non-green at the same time and in the same way. This diversity is destructive, especially in important matters.

If one person affirms that Christ was the preexistent Son of the Father and another denies this same affirma-

---

[5] Pope Paul VI, "True and False Pluralism", *L'Osservatore Romano*, September 5, 1974, p. 1.

[6] Pope Paul VI, "Reconciliation within the Church", *L'Osservatore Romano*, December 26, 1974, p. 2.

tion, one of the two is necessarily out of touch with the reality of God's being and the salvation of the human race. If one person affirms that the vow of poverty taken by religious men and women includes a factual frugality and another denies this, one must be out of touch with what religious life is. There is in contradictions no mutual enrichment, no healthy diversity.

Those who maintain that frequent dissent from the Magisterium is permissible in the Catholic Church need to face squarely and candidly how they are using the term "Catholic". A pluralism in our theology that attempts to justify routine rejection of magisterial teaching and speaks of the rejection as a "Catholic view" is clearly using the term either analogically or equivocally. The word "Catholic" either means something or it does not. Words that mean anything mean nothing. The vast majority of men and women in our society consider that the Catholic Church does stand for something definite in faith and morals, something plainly distinguishable from other religious groups. Despite protestations to the contrary, most people look upon dissenters as dissenters. Whether one is listening to the evening news on television or to two women speaking in the supermarket, one can see that most people do not take seriously the dissenting view as a Catholic teaching. Perhaps those of us who speak and write theology ought to take ourselves less seriously. Others do.

Pope Paul VI repeatedly emphasized that those who depart from magisterial teaching do not speak for the Church. Hence their views are merely private. "No one", said he, "is entitled to accept a label without its contents. This would not be honest. To be a Catholic means to be attached to the Church, a *sincere* and *total* profession of the faith of which she has the deposit, and, therefore, a joyful acceptance of the living magisterium which Christ has conferred on her."[7] In the same vein the papal Secretariat of State, speaking of the World Population Year and the teaching of *Humanae vitae*, asserted that "those who deal with such subjects without heeding the authentic, established teaching cannot claim to represent Catholic viewpoints."[8] Outside a segment of the theological community, few people take seriously the allegation of dissenters that they represent a Catholic position.

Discerning a Healthy Pluralism

We have in this volume sketched the New Testament delineation of a man or woman led by the Holy Spirit. This person has clearly visible traits that identify him as authentic. We find likewise that there are characteristics that indicate when a pluralism in ecclesial life is complementary or contradictory, healthy or unhealthy.

"The body's unity does not do away with the diversity of its members" (CCC 791). A viable diversity is rooted in a shared vision regarding essentials. The New Testament can flourish with its several christological and ecclesial emphases because it does possess one mind about core issues. Although we find diversity explicitly mentioned (for example, 1 Cor 12 and Eph 4), still there is more explicit emphasis on oneness of mind. Paul never tolerated factions and dissensions. For him these were a sign that the community lacked the Holy Spirit, who brings joy, love, peace, harmony (Gal 5:22). Hence the apostle repeatedly pleads that the faithful have one mind and one practice (1

---

[7] November 14, 1968; italics added.
[8] Reported in the *Chicago New World*, February 1, 1974, p. 1.

Cor 1:10f.; Phil 2:1–2; Rom 15:6). The divisions in the Corinthian church are proof that they are not living the gospel; they are still spiritually immature (1 Cor 3:1–3). A rooting in shared vision preserves pluralism from degenerating into fragmentation.

A healthy pluralism possesses boundaries. It is not an amorphous lack of commitment to anything. The Church of the New Testament had limits, and it was the leadership who fixed them. The limits were correct faith and genuine love. The false prophet is known to be false in that he refuses to listen to the leaders of the late-first-century Church (1 Jn 4:1, 6). These "rivals of Christ" never did really belong to the *ekklesia* because they left the community (1 Jn 2:19). Those who reject what they had been taught and seek out another gospel are to be condemned (Gal 1:6–9). The leaders have the power to exclude from the community those who refuse to be corrected and to mend their ways (Mt 18:15–18). We are told that "as there were false prophets in the past history of our people, so you too will have your false teachers, who will insinuate their own disruptive views and disown the Master who purchased their freedom" (2 Pet 2:1). If the Church had no borders, she would be a dull, formless society with nothing to say to the world.

In a vigorous diversity, positions are taken, not on the basis of popularity, but on that of evidence. Prophets do not tailor their message to flatter the desires of their listeners. They do not begin their thinking by considering "what modern men will accept". They know that God's thoughts are not men's, and they expect that many will reject the undiluted message. What has been true among us for centuries seems true also in non-Christian religions: few people accept totality. The argument from polls loses sight of the fact that complete commitment is never popular. Agehanada Bharati, an authority on Eastern religions, has termed counterfeit and spurious the easy, watered-down oriental cults popular among American youth. Most of the gurus in the United States are not accepted by leaders in the East. The few authentic teachers in this country, says Bharati, have not compromised their traditions, and "consequently their followings are small."[9]

The proximate criterion for distinguishing healthy from unhealthy pluralism is the faith of the Church proclaimed in her normative pronouncements. She is the ground and pillar of the truth (1 Tim 3:15). Those who listen to those Jesus sends, listen to him; those who reject them, reject him (Lk 10:16). This criterion could hardly be stated in more express terms.

A complementary pluralism rooted in a shared vision furthers ecclesial unity (Eph 4:11–13). Between contradictions there is no middle ground; one is right and one is wrong. For this reason routine dissent is destructive. Pope Paul VI referred to individual interpretation torn away from apostolic teaching as "indefinitely centrifugal" and as pulverizing the unity of faith.[10]

A healthy pluralism strengthens the Church in her proclamation of the word. A debilitating fragmentation cannot be the work of the Spirit, since he brings unity and strength. Outsiders can hardly take seriously an institution that cannot speak with one clear voice. A maze of opinions impresses no one.

Finite reality is rich, diverse, marvelously variegated. No two twigs are exactly alike, nor are snowflakes, nor

[9] *Detroit Free Press*, February 23, 1974, p. 6-C.
[10] Pope Paul VI, "True and False Pluralism".

are human faces. Yet this diversity demands unity as a condition of its existence. A fractured twig is no longer a twig. A melted snowflake is no snowflake. Separated eyes, noses, mouths are not faces. Factions are not community.

In the moral order, rupture is sin. Sin is rupture. Reality from the very dawn of creation was meant to be in harmony: man with God, man with man, each person within himself. This is why divorce is wrong: it is a division between two who ought to be one flesh in one love. This is why lying is wrong: it is a rupture between minds and persons. This is why lust is wrong: it is a fracture between persons, one of whom at least is using the other as a mere *it*, a thing. This is why atheism is wrong: it sunders man from his only explanation and destiny. Every sin is an unwarranted division.

Contradictory pluralism is a rupture. To speak of pluralism as an invariable good is to indulge in euphemism at best. It is a debilitating destruction at worst. The Church needs a vigorous theology. We need specialists who have pondered the word of God in prayer and then proceed to study it in humble faith and through serious research. We need professionally competent theologians who work within their community and therefore in harmony with those commissioned to articulate the faith to that community. Because there are not two magisteria in the Church, theologians must be humble enough to seek and accept correction, humble enough to learn as well as to teach.

Fragmented theology loses its credibility. Theologians continually at odds with one another and with their own ecclesial community slowly lose their influence. Neither clergy nor laity take them seriously.

Authentic Theology Is Prophetic

No one, be he inclined to the right, left or middle of the theological spectrum, questions the assertion that the Church's proclamation must be vigorous, authentic, prophetic. Almost no one considers debatable the proposition that an amorphous, spineless message attracts and holds no appreciable segment of modern society.

But we have an odd quirk here. The previous paragraph is for the most part theoretical. Rare is the person who would have a problem with it. Yet when we turn the same ideas into the practical realm, universal assent is not forthcoming. Not a little of our proclamation lacks prophetic vigor. One wishes that St. Paul were available to write a weekly column in the diocesan press or to review books in our theological journals. I suspect that my critique of the current dullness would be drab next to his.

I wish here to trace out some of the discerning traits of the biblical prophet as they would apply in our day. We may suppose it to be understood that there are differences between the biblical prophetic office and that of our contemporary theologian. Yet there are striking similarities that cry out for incarnation in living men and women of the twentieth century.

Prophetic theologians are called and sent by the Lord. The divine word originates with the Lord God, not with men. In the old dispensation, the wrath of Yahweh flared up against men who were neither called nor sent by him and yet presumed to speak in his name. This is so true that a contemporary Scripture scholar simply defines the biblical false prophets as "those who speak in their own name (Jer 14:14f.; 23:16), without having been sent (Jer 27:15), following their own inspirations (Ezek 13:3)".[11] The same is true in the new dispensation. As Jesus is sent by the Father, so he sends the structural element in the Church (Jn 20:21). At his command, not their own will, they are to proclaim the word to all creation (Mk 16:15; Mt 28:18–20). It is the Holy Spirit who sets up the overseer bishops to rule the Church of God (Acts 20:28)—they do not appoint themselves.

Authentic theologians are likewise sent. They are not merely acting on their own initiative. This is why priests are to function with faculties from their bishop, are to be in communion with him and through him in communion with the bishop of Rome. Theologically speaking, a priest is an extension of the bishop. He is not something on his own. This is why a priest at odds with his bishop and the Holy See is a theological distortion, an upside-down anomaly.

Because they must be sent, theologians are not a parallel magisterium, a second set of independent teachers in the Church. While bishops should communicate with them and learn from their study and research, it is the hierarchical Magisterium that is normative for theologians, not the other way around. Routine dissent from official teaching is no more permissible in the modern Church than it was in that of St. Paul (cf. Gal 1:6–9 and the pastorals passim). Despite affirmations to the contrary, dissenting theologians are not the Church's theologians. They are private persons speaking in their own names only.

Prophetic theology does not court popularity. Persecution was perhaps the most visible result of authentic prophecy in the Old Testament. And the situation did not change in

---

[11] Paul Beauchamp, in DBT 415.

the new dispensation. Jesus warned the Pharisees that he would send them prophets and wise men and scribes. Some they would slaughter; others they would crucify; still others they would scourge and hunt from town to town (Mt 23:34–36). Those who are faithful to Christ, we read toward the end of the first century, are certain to be persecuted (2 Tim 3:12).

Current argumentation from polls in matters of moral conduct tacitly supposes the expectation that most men will accept gospel morality. It loses sight of the fact that Jesus had plainly said that few would enter the narrow gate and tread the hard road of his moral code (Mt 7:13–14). It forgets Paul's warning to the Thessalonians that they must expect rejection and persecution (1 Th 3:4). There is something suspect about a moral norm that is generally acceptable. No prophet in the old dispensation and surely neither Jesus nor the apostles in the new tailored their moral demands to what the majority were willing to accept. When there was a clash between teaching and living (and there were many), it was the living that was to change, not the teaching. A moral theology that "tends to follow middle-class mores rather than the New Testament"[12] is not discerning the mind of God.

Prophetic theology is committed to something definite and sure. Scepticism is an intellectual disease. The human intellect is made to mirror reality, to come to grips with what is. An inability to leave off questioning once sufficient evidence is present and to come to a firm assent is an intellectual neurosis. It is perhaps even more akin to an intellectual suicide. A mind that suspends judgment about everything commits itself to nothing. We see among religious con-

[12] Paul Hanly Furfey and Norbert J. Rigali, *National Catholic Reporter*, February 14, 1975, p. 19.

gregations that those who hold to nothing distinctive, who are continually "searching" but never finding, are dissolving before our very eyes. Many leave; few enter. It takes little perceptivity to discern the illness. Theological scepticism is intimately linked to dissent from magisterial teaching. That this is not an unfounded judgment may be seen in a recent statement that "the ultimate theological reason for the possibility of dissent from specific moral teachings comes from the impossibility of achieving absolute certitude in the light of the complex elements involved in *any* specific moral judgment or teaching."[13] This seems to imply a moral scepticism, since in this view absolute certitude in *any* specific moral judgment or teaching is impossible. If one seriously holds this position, some interesting conclusions follow.

There then seems little need for moral theologians. Sceptical positions when they become universal tend to do away with the field in which no certitude is possible. At the very least it becomes difficult to take the practitioners of that field seriously, for in principle one always has the right to reject what they say as unfounded.

This position is foreign to the mind of the biblical prophets. St. Paul, too, gives every impression of teaching and deciding definitively what was and what was not morally in accord with the good news. One may not respond to this observation by saying that things were more simple in those days. They were, of course, in some ways but not in all. Nonetheless, the sceptical position deals with any specific moral judgment or teaching, and that obviously includes simple ones.

[13] Charles E. Curran, "Is There a Catholic and/or Christian Ethic?" *Catholic Theological Society of America Proceedings*, 1974, p. 151; italics added.

A noncertitude position renders moral guidance of the faithful almost impossible, whether that guidance is given from the pulpit, in the classroom or in the sacrament of reconciliation. If the opposite teaching always has some likelihood of being correct, one would be either arrogant or irresponsible in giving a definite, straightforward answer to a specific ethical question. One needs little imagination to picture what would happen to most people's thinking if they were taught that any moral judgment may or may not be true.

Moral scepticism is surely rejected by the Magisterium itself. Through the centuries and in our own day, the Church's teaching office gives the clear impression of presenting morality with a serene certitude.

Prophetic theology is faithful to its tradition. In an earlier chapter we saw that a sure mark of the true prophet is that he is faithful to known revelation. Deuteronomy 13:1–6 is a classical statement of the biblical conviction that even if a man works a miracle, he is a false prophet if his teaching is false. We noted how the most explicit discernment text in all Scripture makes the same point: The true prophet listens to the Church's teaching, the false does not (1 Jn 4:1–6).

So it is to this day. The authentic theologian is hopefully concerned with the problems of his day, does his research carefully and thoroughly, is perceptive and creative in his thought. But he is also faithful to his tradition. He does not reinterpret the core content of a doctrine into an unrecognizable departure from what it has always meant. His work may not make headlines, but it does make Christians.

Prophetic theology is prayerful. One of the outstanding weaknesses of much (not all) of current moral theology is its technician approach, that is, its viewing moral acts in isolation from their goal, an immersion in God through an interpersonal relationship of love and prayer begun on earth and consummated in beatific love in a risen body. Vatican Council II reminded us of what we have long known in our theology (but not always practiced), namely, that in the Church action is subordinated to contemplation and is directed to it (SC no. 2). This simple statement, once it is taken seriously, is explosive in its consequences.

A prophetic theologian does take it seriously. He deals with human actions, not as mere means, not as isolated happenings, but as interpersonal relations with a beloved. He sees buying, selling, playing, digging, cooking, building, not as mere interhuman matters, but also as part of a whole life-style penetrated with a singing to the Lord in one's heart "always and everywhere" (Eph 5:19 20)—and subordinated to that singing. And more, he shows how building and cooking and playing are orientated to the contemplation both of earth and of heaven.

A nonprophetic theologian proclaims a morality of means. He can lecture hour after hour, write article after article and scarcely ever relate social justice or genetics with a prayerful communion with God. Yet this morality of means is like a man driving from Boston to Phoenix and thinking only of fuel, tires, maps and motels and never reflecting on his beloved whom he is to visit.

We need profoundly to return to our biblical and patristic origins so that we might understand anew that our daily actions are part of a whole life-style that is intimately related to our prayer. St. Paul does not deal with action in one place and then severely separate it from prayer in another. The patristic giants (for example, Ignatius of Antioch, Origen, Gregory of Nyssa, Ambrose, Augustine, Gregory the Great) intimately mingled their ethical thoughts with prayerful reflections. They would have considered many of our moral tracts as sterile and impersonal and merely human.

The Call of a Sure Trumpet

One hardly needs to prove that amidst the pervasive insecurities and disillusionments of our age men and women are eager to hear the call of a clear and sure trumpet. Good people are looking for saints and prophets, not for mere weavers of words. They desire ecclesial leadership to lead securely to the mind of the Lord God and not merely to a welter of human opinions. The man who works with his hands for a living is not a sceptic—he is too healthy—and he is not happy with a doubting leadership.

On the natural plane we speak of the growing unity of the human race at least from the point of view of communications. With the advent of the space age we now have in pictures taken from the moon a symbol of our global village. According to the mind of Jesus, the Church is to signify in her very life the union of men among themselves and with God (Jn 17:23; 1 Jn 1:3). To do this authentically, she cannot be rent with doctrinal divisions or serious disciplinary dissensions. This sacramentality of the Church requires an inner harmony and consistency of doctrine, life and worship. This trait of the apostolic Church was so central that Luke summarizes the health of the ideal early *ekklesia* by saying that the faithful were committed to the one proclamation of the apostles, to the community, to the Eucharist and to prayer (Acts 2:42). Such is the home of the Spirit.

INDEX

preoccupation with, 115–
19, 118n. 30
types of communication,
62, 70–74
origin of, 61–62, 93–95
as privilege, 74–76, 113
See also experience; religious
experience

faith, 237
growth in, 28, 121–22, 248
and preoccupation with
divine messages, 117–19
relationship to intellect and
reason, 95–96
Feuillet, André,
"La Morale chrétienne
d'après Saint Jean", 240–
41n. 3
Fitzmyer, Joseph A.,
in Jerome Biblical Commentary, 48n. 19, 218n. 5
Forestell, J. Terence,
in Jerome Biblical Commentary, 192n. 4
formal locutions, 73
See also locutions
Francis of Assisi, St., 202,
223
Fransen, Piet, 61, 92, 201
freedom from attachment.
See detachment
free will, 60, 69

conclusions based on, 183–
84, 205
errors as expression of, 36,
38, 189–94
and faith, 196, 237
frugality, 165–66
life-style of, 33, 168–69, 202
as sign of authenticity, 154–
58, 168–69
Futrell, John, 41

George, Augustin,
in Dictionary of Biblical Theology, 48n. 19
gnosis,
definition of, 84–85
God-directedness, 147–49
goodness. See holiness;
peace-joy
gospel morality,
discernment as key to, 234–
39
pagan morality vs., 239–42
and two views of morality,
232–34
Gospel Paradox, The (Javelet),
192–93n. 4
Grassi, Joseph A.,
in Jerome Biblical Commentary, 161n. 3
Greek Orthodox Theological
Review, The,
"Tradition in the New Tes-

of Christians vs. of pagans,
239–42
norms in, 37, 240
scepticism, 256–59
signs of authenticity in,
143–44
cross-asceticism, 152–54
frugality, 154–59
God-directedness, 144–49,
145–46n. 2
new love, 149–52
See also gospel morality
moral conversion, 199–201
See also conversion
Moran, W. L., 107n. 20
More, St. Thomas, 28
motivation, unconscious,
choices based on, 15, 143,
200–201
definition of, 43, 85, 193
Murray, John Courtney, 199
Mussner, Franz, 161
The Epistle to the Colossians,
48n. 19
Mystical Body model of the
Church, 247
mystics, 43, 139–40
definition of, 58n. 3
on individual experiences of
God, 62–69
sobriety of, 87–90
*See also names of individual
mystics*

natural resources and frugal-
ity, 155–56
nature of man. *See* human
nature
New Blackfriars,
"Objections to Lonergan's
Method" (Kerr), 202n. 9
*New Catholic Commentary on
Holy Scripture, A*,
Cardinal Bea in, 176n. 4
Byrne in, 192–93n. 4
Dalton in, 164n. 9
O'Curraoin in, 192–93n. 4
O'Rourke in, 226n. 12
R. Russell in, 164n. 7
Theissen in, 192–93n. 4
Wansbrough in, 48n. 19
New Catholic Encyclopedia,
Pegon in, 177n. 7
"Prophetism (in the Bible)",
160n. 1
*New Testament for Spiritual
Reading*,
The Acts of the Apostles
(Kurzinger), 48n. 19
The Epistle to the Colossians
(Mussner), 48n. 19
The Epistle to the Ephesians
(Zerwick), 48n. 19
The Epistle to the Galatians
(Schneider), 161n. 2
The Epistle to Titus (Reuss),
48n. 19

Rousseau, Jean-Jacques, 145–
46n. 2
Russell, Bertrand, 145–46n. 2
Russell, Ralph,
in *A New Catholic Commentary on Holy Scripture*,
164n. 7

Sabourin, Leopold, 93–94
sacrament of Christ model of
the Church, 246
saints, 153
authenticity of, 27–30
discernment of, 25, 32, 233–
36
frugality of, 157–58
sobriety of, 87–90, 147
See also holiness
Sartre, Jean-Paul, 145–46n. 2
Satan. *See* devil
scepticism, 244, 256–58
Schelkle, Karl, 106n. 17
Schleiermacher, Friedrich,
83–84, 96
Schnackenburg, Rudolf, 47,
177, 178
Schneider, Gerhard, 48
The Epistle to the Galatians,
161n. 2
Schwank, Benedikt,
The First Epistle of Peter,
48n. 19, 177n. 6, 178n. 9
secularism, 145–46n. 2

self-denial, 165–66
sensual pleasures,
in descriptions of experiences of God, 63–64, 66,
68–69, 148
preoccupation with, 168–70,
237–38
and sexual morality of the
gospel, 237–38
Simon, Yves, 229
simplicity and humility, 125–
27
sin,
as cause of darkness, 186–89,
194, 200, 201
definition of, 187
influence of, 92–93, 153
relationship to,
division, 253
errors, 36, 91–93
pride, 128
repentance, 194–95
unrepentance, 113, 191–
92, 194
See also errors
situation ethics, 85–86
sobriety of mystics, 32, 87–90,
147, 189
society. *See* world
Society of Jesus, 179–80,
222n. 9
Solzhenitsyn, Alexander,
192–93

Theissen, A.,
in *A New Catholic Commentary on Holy Scripture*,
192–93n. 4
Theological Dictionary of the New Testament (Kittel),
"*Diakrino, Diakrisis*"
(Buechsel), 102n. 2
"*Dokimos*" (Grundmann),
102n. 2
theology, 188
authority as influence on,
230–31
doctrinal fidelity in current
times, 165–66, 185–86
paths in, 240–42, 245
as prophetic, 254–60
and scepticism, 256–58
See also doctrines
Therrien, Gerard,
*Discernement dans les écrits
pauliniens, Le*, 16, 102n. 2
Thomas Aquinas, St., 40, 67
Thusing, Wilhelm, 104
Timothy, St., 162, 165, 227–28
Titus, St., 162
Tolstoy, Leo, 145–46n. 2
Trilling, Wolfgang,
*The Gospel according to St.
Matthew*, 192n. 4
on holiness, 129, 155
on pertinacity of sinners,
113, 195

Truhlar, K. V., 146–47
truth, 14, 143
attainment of, 182–83
biblical explanations, 186–98
fullness of conversion, 204
intellectual conversion,
198–99
moral conversion, 199–201
person-centered knowledge, 182, 183
problems, 183–86, 205–7
religious conversion, 201–3
research-study model,
182–83
in errors, 34, 39, 51, 90–91,
91n. 12
in human nature, 26–27
and illuminism, 51–53
as located in consciousness,
83–84
and roots of illusion, 35–38
See also authenticity; knowledge

unconscious motivation. *See*
motivation, unconscious
unity, 243
Paul on, 106n. 17, 173,
173n. 1, 174, 215, 248
as sign of authentic community, 49, 172–75